Who Is Destroying Your Future?

Taking back control of our lives,
our money and our future

John H. Zaugg

Turning the lights back on in America

Contents

One:

What is "good" & "right"?

> Nothing is to be taken for granted, especially not if it is handed down by an authority which puts itself above the moral reasoning of the people, be that putative authority in the form of Zeus or of a human tyrant. Every man must work out for himself what is good and right, and nobody can escape the obligation of examining himself and his life.
> — Socrates, 630 BC

Socrates is defining the challenge that we all face to make life a positive experience achieving the goals and self confidence we should be striving for. Unfortunately things are not going well. So let's start the process of examining ourselves and our culture to define what is *good* and *right*.

We are faced with challenges unlike anything in our recent history. The revival of our prospects and confidence will require two things. First, in order to solve a problem we have to define the underlying cause of the problem. Second, we have to forge a new path that is built on what is *good* and *right*; and start holding accountable those leading us down the path into self-destruction. Both of these essential steps means restoring our "vision" of how to achieve the confidence and meaning that life should be all about. Defining the "vision" that should guild us, will put an end to reliance on authoritarian subservience and inspire us to build or lives on personal convictions.

Before starting the discussion write a short essay to answer the question: ***Who is destroying your future***? Does anyone from your grandparents to parents and school teachers give you confidence in the future they are preparing you for? Is the American political system keeping the promises that it made over two hundred years ago? Do our politicians, conservative or progressive, have a plan that will inspire and achieve any of the promises they make? The purpose of this essay is for you to take a look at yourself and the world you now live in and endure.

Now, let's start the discussion.

What has gone wrong? When I was growing up my parents didn't keep our home locked up or the car locked when parked on the street. Now here in Denver one in three homes has a steel security door on the entrance. Instead of growing peace, prosperity and confidence we have just the opposite; growing apprehension, poverty and distrust.

I think the underlying problem started clear back in the 1930s. That was when we changed course from a nation dedicated and built on personal responsibility into a nation reliant on benevolent government. Over the decades we have been mislead and indoctrinated into believing that *government* should and would care for all our problems better than relying on citizens to exercise basic responsibilities. Reliance on collective obedience has been the path we have chosen. Clearly it's not working.

Instead of mandatory obedience, what parents and grandparents should be saying to their children is that everything they do is all about your future. We are paying off the mortgage on our home, we are putting money into a saving account to give you inheritance benefits to assure you a path to financial security, we are building on the values that assures world peace and prosperity to make everyone's future safe and secure and we are providing you with the education essential to make the most of your life. That should be every parent's mission and promise. Instead parents are running up the national debt, living on Social Security, taking out a reverse mortgage so when they die they leave nothing for their children.

What we are doing with benevolent government and military spending is putting our children and grandchildren ever deep in debt. We are sucking the life blood out of our children's future. It is destroying future generation's hope of any kind of enduring financial security or meaningful respect for everyone. Government has become the institution we are all supposed to rely on. We are treating people like doormats and obedient subjects. We must start to talk about what has to change.

The problem is mandatory subservience

Social Security is the just one piece of evidence of our reliance on authoritarian subservience. Social Security is like the canary in the coal mine. The canary is gasping for life as long as we continue to deceive ourselves about what has gone wrong and has to change. But just demanding less government won't solve the problem.

Reliance on government is why we are now witnessing the growing loss of hope, the growing disparity, violence and poverty. A vast majority of Americans think social security is the greatest thing since the invention of toilet paper. Instead it is evidence of how we are failing our children by abandoning and betraying the essential respect for people and those essential shared convictions about what kind of nation we should be building. We have abandoned government that respects and protects our rights and liberties and instead have gone down a path into a massive bureaucratic authoritarian state. We have abandoned or redefined our convictions to what is *good* and *right* to bring to an end our reliance on corrupt government and end our addiction to bad habits.

In a *free society* each takes responsibility for their life. In an *authoritarian state* people live as subjects of the government. That is what we are now enduring, living as a nation of obedient subjects. This brings us to the question: If servitude is the problem how do we restore confidence and convictions that will keep the promise that America was supposed to stand proudly for?

Most young people are well aware that their future is in jeopardy. Is there a basis for genuine hope that is real and achievable? The answer to that question is: **YES.**

Here is an example to illustrate that there is indeed an alternative—a *good* and *right* path that we could be taking.

A fourth grade class has just completed a lesson on American history. The students loved the information and wanted more of the materials they were studying. At the end of the class the teacher asks if there are any questions. Immediately several students put their hands up. They want to talk. The teacher goes from one to the next to address their questions. Then she comes to a new student in the school, Catherine.

The room grows quiet and Catherine asks her question. The question was: I am a new student in your school and I am impressed by the subjects and the comprehension that you address and convey. But, as a new student I have a question about this school and about the what "America" represents and the meaning of the US Constitution that you were discussing.

After several years of home schooling my parents enrolled me in this school. I'm curious why they sent me here and what kind of education I can expect here. For example, when I finally start a job I am going to be required by law to pay taxes to fund all those welfare programs and retirement benefits such as Social Security.

As you were describing this was supposed to be the land of the free. As specified in the Constitution, I and all my fellow classmates are supposed to have an absolute, inalienable right to our life, liberty and pursuit of happiness. In my opinion government welfare, subsidies and handouts are a gross violation of the principles set forth by a free society. So my question is: Does this school teach the values that would fulfill the rights and liberties that America was supposed to stand for? Can I expect the truth and the respect we all deserve?

The teacher went silent for a moment because this is the first time she had any idea what kind of attitude and determination Catherine was going to bring to her class room. Then she addressed Catherine's question.

The answer is "yes" we are going to revere and teach the values that freedom and humanity must be built upon.

Let me address your question. We are a private not a public school that abides by the rules and regulation set forth by government. There are no security guards at this school. You will never be threatened if you disagree with our education policies. We want you to stand-up and become a person of character. In fact the way we promote safety, security and respect here is by the only means that personal safety will ever be achieved, by learning to talk to everyone with *honesty* and *respect*. The school shootings that you have all heard about would never have occurred if respect for and talking to one another had been part of those schools. A person of character does not ignore or turn their backs on the people around them. Our mission is to do the right thing. There will be no government mandated testing. There is no government mandated curriculum to indoctrinate you. There will be no junk food in our cafeteria. There will be no discrimination based on a person's views, convictions, race, sex, or even how they dress. We are committed to one objective—to give every student the convictions, education, and support to become the best they choose to become, to define and reach their goals in life. Understanding what we all shared in common means talking about those core values.

We now live in a culture of mindless consumers and couch potatoes that live as servants of parasitic government. Our goal is to enable you to be the new leaders. For example, to answer your question about Social Security, we are going to recommend that you insist that politicians bring an end to Social Security and all federal welfare programs. You can lead the world to build the enduring peace and prosperity that we should all be working for. For example, the Amish refuse to pay SS taxes or accept any benefits; they support their families, care for the elderly, eat healthy foods and do not pollute the environment. In sixty years when you reach retirement you will have ended Social Security and you will have forged and whole new vision for America that is built on personal convictions instead of forced obedience. You will refuse to buy a car that runs on fossil fuels, refuse to eat foods laced with chemicals, and refuse to use electricity generated by coal, natural gas, fossil fuels or nuclear energy. We are going to teach you how you can grow all the food your family will need with your own garden and green house. We will be teaching you how to provide all the electricity for your home. We are also going to address and talk about your personal choices when faced with the questions of family values, social responsibility and population growth. We are going to talk about the values and long range commitments necessary to build a bright future. Here at this school, your future is the focus of our attention.

We will be addressing the three major threats to your future. The first being printing money that is destroying the middle class and causing increasing poverty; second, deficit spending that is destroying your prospects for a future of financial security; and third, the military-industrial-corporate complex that leads us into bankruptcy and ever increasing terrorism.

Let's be honest—the reason public schools are so silent about those essential moral values is because if they taught such values it would expose just how corrupt our current leadership has become. What you are going to learn is how to make the most of your life instead of living as subjects of authoritarian ideologies. You will learn how to live dedicated to exercising personal convictions knowing what "good" and "right" means and requires. We welcome you and look forward to answering any questions you will bring to our attention.

Catherine now knew why her parents had chosen this school.

How to become part of the solution

I am in my seventies and have witnessed what has happened over the past sixty years that is so completely un-necessary. The ongoing destruction has been malicious and deliberate—a matter of public policy. The underlying problem is the total absence of competent leadership. Instead of leadership we endure a system that insists that people live as obedient subjects. THE ALTERNATIVE means we define a genuine, realizable moral compass to guide our lives and social norms to function as free, independent and competent adults. It means government that serves its essential function—to respect and protect everyone's rights and be there for people and the community in an emergency. That means we don't live in a welfare state or throw people into prison believing such public policies are going to solve the growing crime or poverty problems. Solutions require schools that teach and discuss the convictions that addresses and solve problems instead of being taught to live as obedient subjects.

The guiding purpose and goal of all our lives should be to leave the world a better place. This means everything we do, how we deal with every challenge we face, how we care for our loved ones, our friends, our fellow workers, and our community—with every choice our goal is to solve the problems we are confronted with to build a better future. That is our moral obligation. When we ignore, remain silent, or compromise or make excuses to avoid that moral imperative we are the problem. The core values that give substance and meaning to living and working together as *problem solvers* are *honesty* and *respect*. These values are not complicated but, unfortunately today, they are ignored and replaced with lies, scams, and contempt for everyone.

When I was growing up the subject of moral values was never part of public education. You would think in a nation dedicated and founded on historic ideals, those ideals would be taught in our schools. Well guess what. From grade school all the way through college we were taught to live in a moral fog dependent on top down management. That is the underlying problem. It is also evidence of why this subject about ethics and morality will not be popular with today's adults. This is a discussion millions of Americans do not what to engage in. So be forewarned that this is a subject that you're reading about, probably for the first time. There are numerous books, authors, professors, commentators, adults who will teach and talk about moral values but they are deliberately misleading us. Their only mission is to maintain the status-quo, motivated by the quest for power, subsidies and profits. They promise over and over to fix the problems, from economic disparity, violence, mediocre education, national security, drug abuse, the environmental crisis and the problems only remain and grow worse. Some of us are beginning to wake up.

Let me start with what I observed back when I was growing up that were deliberately being perpetuated by our incompetent leaders.

Here is an example of what has gone so wrong. The war on drugs was enacted under Emperor Richard Nixon (1971) but we can't blame Nixon. The war on drugs was passed by democrats and republicans and has had their full support and funding for forty years. The promise was to solve the growing drug abuse problems. It was just another scam. The intent of the war on drugs was to raise the power of authoritarian governing. It has put a million citizens, mostly poor and minorities, into our prison system, has cost taxpayers billions and has accomplished exactly nothing except to encourage drug consumption, benefit the corporate prison complex, and motivate the illegal drug cartels within and outside the US. And the incompetent leaders have NO intention of ending this immoral and criminal, authoritarian scam. For them this is what governing is all about, the use of force to solve a problem which has exactly the opposite consequence. Why anyone who takes being human and personal responsibility seriously would vote for or support a *democratic* or *republican* politician is beyond comprehension. The point is we are a nation wearing blinders and this blindness was no accident. You, the next generation, has to forge a new path and over throw the existing System.

Evidence of the scam is everywhere

I can remember back when I was growing up, I never heard anyone talk about needing health insurance. Probably because people were healthy and health care was so inexpensive and available that doctors made house calls. And, back then, one working parent could support the family including health care. Today it takes two working parents and they may need multiple jobs. And the children are raised in childcare facilities. But that was also when manufactured junk foods became popular and the health crisis has been growing ever since. Manufacture foods contain little nutritional value and are laced with ingredients that make then taste good so we become addicted to them. We are witnessing the obesity, diabetes and heart disease that are the consequence. It's just more evidence of the mindless consumerism, DUH, that by evading personal responsibly we end up relying on a bunch of chemicals, misleading advertising, bad habits, manufact- ured drugs and government welfare. The pollution of the air we breathe, the foods we eat and the water we drink got started with the industrial revolution poisoning the environment and resulted in the growing deterioration of our well being including the growing cancer and mental disorders. Today, children are coming down with cancer. It's like living in a warehouse with no windows, polluted air and reliance on force is the only solution to our problems. And the emperors up on stage promise they are fixing the disparity, poverty, and health crisis. It's not a democracy, it's not a republic, it's a scam.

Here is a revolutionary idea, health care should be paid for by those who are making us all sick—who produce, emit, advertise, and sell poisonous chemicals including, for example, auto manufactures who produce cars that run on fossil fuels. Those who commit a crime should pay for the damages they cause. But this is not about the corruption and clearly government isn't going to solve the problem. We have to stop buying into their lies. We have to stop buying the products poisoning the environment—the air we breath, the water we drink, the foods we eat.

> Drinking water supplies for more than six million Americans contain unsafe levels of industrial chemicals that have been linked to cancer and other serious health problems, a U.S. study suggests.
> The chemicals – known as PFASs (for polyfluoroalkyl and perfluoroalkyl substances) – are used in products ranging from food wrappers to clothing to nonstick cookware to fire-fighting foams. They have been linked with an increased risk of kidney and testicular cancers, hormone disruption, high cholesterol, and obesity.
> — Lisa Rapaport, Reuters Health (2016)

Here is a story (typical back in 1990-2007) to illustrate both the underlying flaw and the solution to the pervasive corruption.

The CEO of a very large banking institution has returned to his office. He is manager of the mortgage division of this bank. He stops at the desk of his secretary to get the agenda for the day. His secretary who has been working with him for years lays out his schedule for him and then tells him: *We received a memorandum that I put on your desk.*

The CEO goes into his office and reads the memoranda. It's a proposal to revise bank lending policies to increase profitability. It recommends this bank should offer mortgages with no proof of earning or income, with no money down, with artificially low adjustable rate mortgages, and mortgages will be guaranteed through new government lending institutions called Fannie May and Freddie Mac. (The more recent example of government mortgage financing programs would be something called HARP)

After reading the memo the CEO calls his secretary into his office. He says to her: *Get me a list of all those who prepared these suggested new lending policies.* She replies: *I am already working on it. They are all going to be fired aren't they.*

The CEO responds: *I hired these executives because I trusted them. I didn't hire them to scam our customers. It is my job to manage the mortgage division of this vitally important banking institution. If these banking policies and government guarantees became standard policies it would eventually bring down the whole banking system. I will not be part of such corruption.*

For lack of such integrity we were lead into financial collapse of 2008. We are told, over and over by the emperors that the solution is government regulation of banks and bailouts of financial institutions too-big-to-fail. But the "truth" was never acknowledged, that the problem is a lack of basic moral convictions. People of integrity would not tolerate corruption and organized shenanigans. Government has no right to use working citizen's earnings to bail out the corrupt banking institutions, and then allows million dollar bonuses for CEO's.

Parents go to the bank they have been doing business with to apply for a home mortgage. The mortgage advisor tells them they have come at the right time. They can get a mortgage with no proof of earning, with no money down, low adjustable rate mortgages, and the government will guarantee mortgages for financially deficient Americans.

These *responsible* parents look at each other, laugh out loud, and get up and leave. They know a fraud when they see one. Within two weeks they have removed all accounts with this bank and have moved to a locally owned bank that promised to exercise basic integrity. They know that financial institutions that gamble with their customer's money and encourage their customers to play the System are nothing but casinos. These responsible adults feel sorry for those who have been indoctrinated into relying on fancy excuses; but, based on their convictions they take the necessary steps to protect their family. That is the difference between those who live on fancy excuses verses those who recognize the need for meaningful convictions and taking responsibility for their finances, welfare and families.

We need a banking system that is regulated by government, for example, that prohibit banks from using their customer's money to invest in speculative derivatives; and a banking system that practices an explicit commitment to handle customer's money so that it is virtually guaranteed to be protected from fraud and speculative gambling. A banking system based on the exercise of genuine commitment to integrity.

That is how a free society must function to achieve the lasting financial security that we should expect of ourselves. Prior to the 2008 financial collapse did you hear one financial expert warn us about the coming collapse? Did you hear anyone warn home buyers of the scams they were being lead into by the banks and government financial services?

There are two underlying causes for the economic disparity and looming financial collapse. One, the federal reserve that was supposed to protect and assure the integrity of our currency, and second, the massive size and cost of our government funding the socialist/capitalist System that is out of control. Let's start with one of the biggest scams—the FED.

We now live in a nation that has abandoned any meaningful regard for principles or values, a nation that lives in a moral fog that is deliberately instituted and manipulated by the Emperors up on stage. Perhaps the best example is the deliberate manipulation of our currency. Just to be clear, our "currency" is what we use to exchange goods and services—that keeps bread on the table for every family. The corruption of our currency is the root cause for the growing poverty and ultimately leads to the destruction of the middle class.

> This Act (the Federal Reserve Act, Dec. 23rd 1913) establishes the most gigantic trust on earth. When the President signs this bill, the invisible government by the Monetary Power will be legalized. The people may not know it immediately, but the day of reckoning is only a few years removed. The trusts will soon realize that they have gone too far even for their own good. The people must make a declaration of independence to relieve themselves from the Monetary Power. This they will be able to do by taking control of Congress. Wall Streeters could not cheat us if you Senators and Representatives did not make a humbug of Congress... The greatest crime of Congress is its currency system. The worst legislative crime of the ages is perpetrated by this banking bill. The caucus and the party bosses have again operated and prevented the people from getting the benefit of their own government.
> — Charles A. Lindbergh, Sr. (1859-1924) Congressman (R-MN), father of famous aviator. Source:

December 22, 1913, the day before President Woodrow Wilson signed the Federal Reserve Act, in a speech before the House of Representatives.

Inflation has now been institutionalized at a fairly constant 5% per year. This has been determined to be the optimum level for generating the most revenue without causing public alarm. A 5% devaluation applies, not only to the money earned this year, but to all that is left over from previous years. At the end of the first year, a dollar is worth 95 cents. At the end of the second year, the 95 cents is reduced again by 5%, leaving its worth at 90 cents, and so on. By the time a person has worked 20 years, the government will have confiscated 64% of every dollar he saved over those years. By the time he has worked 45 years, the hidden tax will be 90%. The government will take virtually everything a person saves over a lifetime.
— G. Edward Griffin, American Historian, Author

The Federal Reserve should be abolished because it is immoral, unconstitutional, impractical, promotes bad economics, and undermines liberty. Its destructive nature makes it a tool of tyrannical government.
— Ron Paul, *End the FED* (2009)

To illustrate just how corrupt money and our government has become consider the wars in Iraq and Afghanistan. They cost a trillion dollars, or more, and continue to run up more debt. These wars were never authorized by the Congress as required in our constitution. Emperor President Bush said to congress, "You either support this war or I will proceed with it under my authority." But even more corrupt, did our politicians raise taxes to pay for these wars? No, they borrowed the money putting future generation into more debt and printed the money which is why we endure increasing inflation, poverty and disparity requiring raising the minimum wage because current wages do not pay for basic necessities. The fiat (printed) money allows our government to get away with endless scams and corruption.

Do our politicians make any apologies? No, they claim that sending our youth into needless wars is good for us, patriotic and justifies the massive spending and debt. They sacrificed thousands of America's finest and murdered thousands of people for no good reason. It's totally immoral. None of these wars were necessary to protector or defend the United States and actually made the world and America less safe.

> Prophets are not those who speak of piety and duty from the pulpits—there are few people in pulpits worth listening to. The prophets are the battered wrecks of men and women who return from Iraq and find the courage to speak the halting words we do not want to hear, words we must hear and digest in order to know ourselves. These veterans, the ones who dare to tell the truth, have seen and tasted how war plunges us into barbarity, perversion, pain, and an unchecked orgy of death. And it is their testimonies, if we take the time to listen, which alone can save us.
> — Chris Hedges, *The World As It Is: Dispatches on the myth of Human Progress*, (2001)

Today's massive government extortion and politicians that fund the military/corporate complex are taking future generations into poverty. It's beyond belief and comprehension. And ultimately it is our fault because we let they get away with it. It's like living in a country run by the mafia. Article Section 8 of the US Constitution defines the role and responsibilities of Congress, *"To declare war.*" The president is supposed to manage the military, not take us into wars. If the members of congress ignore the Constitution that they took an oath to up hold then why do we keep re-electing them? Could it be because they promise us free rides, endless consumption, welfare, tax loop-holes, subsidies, hope and change? Are we really that gullible? Apparently! (See ***The Empire Has No Clothes*** by Ivan Eland)

Evidence of the problem for me started back in the 60's while I was still in college. I was attending Ohio State University. One day I attended an anti-war rally. There must have been a couple of hundred students there, all standing in the meeting hall. I noticed standing around the back of the room some men wearing black trench coats. They were clearly not students. They were probably government agents spying on us protesters. I and some of my friends were drafted out of college. I managed to avoid military service, many did not and were force to serve, but the oppression was clear. A couple of years later at Kent State University (1970) there were student on the college campus protesting against the Viet Nam War, and the dictators sent national-guard units with military weapons onto the campus. They open fire seventy feet away from the protestors and assassinated four students (two of which were protesters). To learn more about this deliberate killing go to Wikipedia. We are a nation disgusted with our government, but we continue to tolerate the corruption and get lead down the same slippery slope.

What was never reported is that needless assaults on innocent people, perpetrated by our government, was and remains evidence of what has gone so wrong in America. Any government, law enforcement or nation that would send armed police or military personal onto a college campus is a culture living in a moral fog. Any nation that would drop bombs on people for no justifiable reason, is a nation that does not revere or teach basic moral values. We have to wake up. We live in a culture where the only solution that our emperors know to address or solve a problem is the use of force. It represents a path into humanitarian collapse. It has only gotten worse as evidence by the growing domestic violence, meaningless debates, phony solutions and obsession with needless wars.

There is an alternative.

We could have police and law enforcement that we admire, respect and trust

A few years ago the 99% protesters were expressing their contempt of Wall Street and the special interests that are destroying the middle class and causing the growing poverty. The protestors were in many cities including here in Denver. I went down to Civic Center Park one day to witness first hand their protest movement. They had tents set up, tables of handouts for those interested in their ideas and views, and a library with a hundred books for those who wanted to expand their knowledge and awareness. They were very welcoming to anyone who wanted to share in the discussion and views about what was happening to America.

Then a week or more later, in the dark of night, the police showed up, threw all the protesters out of Civic Center Park and confiscated all of their belongings loading them on to trash removal trucks. That was the end of the protests. The rulers had accomplished their mission. It's just another example that the only solution that democrats and republicans have to address a problem is the use of force and the problems only grow worse. They did not respect these citizens; they did not want to talk to these people or even acknowledge that they deserved any respect. It's evidence of the ongoing, insidious contempt for people.

What if the police when ordered to remove the protesters had refused to obey because their mission, their job, was supposed to be *to respect and protect the rights and liberties of all citizens*. Or, better yet, **what if** they shown up at Civic Center Park and set down and talked to the protesters. Then after they had expressed and shared their humanity they could have shook hands and hugged the protesters and left. They probably would have been fired from their jobs for refusal to obey their superiors. Then they and the community could have joined in protests about the violations, brutality and betrayal of the principles that our Constitution and America is supposed to represent and that the government was supposed to uphold and defend. That is how we will restore trust and respect for our police and government. **Standing up** for what is *good* and *right* is how we solve problems. It is the only way we will restore any genuine hope for our future.

Here is a more recent evidence of the blindness. After the Dallas shooting that killed five police officers and wounded seven others I watched the news, commentary and interviews about this tragedy (*This Week with George Stephanopoulos, Meet the Press, Face the Nation, Democracy Now, MSNBC, PBS, President Obama, Hillary Clinton & Donald Trump*). Lots of talk about how devastating, horrific and not what America stands for; BUT, not once did I hear anyone talk about the underlying causes of the growing violence, distrust, and hopelessness. Never acknowledged is that we now live in what is more and more a repressive system, militarized policing, reliance on forced obedience that is degenerating into a failed state. This is not the fault of incompetent police. It is the *System* that promotes the reliance on brute force to solve every problem and more and more people are disgusted, fed-up and rebelling.

Young people your future is being destroyed by democrats, republicans, mediocre education and the nonsense being touted by college professors and talking heads. Today's commentators promote the partisan debate (gridlock) and at the same time, remain silent about what must change.

How much time and attention do you spend considering the kind of person you are? Are you part of the solution or part of the problem? When was the last time you had a discussion about the values on which everyone's success depends? Are you confident we are building a better future for the next generation? Do you view brute force (laws, obedience, subsidies and welfare) as what citizens must rely upon? Now go back and read your essay about who you think is destroying your future. Did you define the underlying problem and/or the solution?

I have read numerous books on ethics, philosophy and analysis of the many deficiencies in our culture, but what's lacking are any specific expectations to resolve and end the growing apprehension. There is no such thing as middle ground or compromise that will save us from the next crisis. In fact most of those authors predict that the next crisis is coming. It isn't just that the current path and grid-lock is a failure, but we persist in this nonsense with no intention of restoring personal accountability and constitutional government. How mediocre does our public education have to descend before we get serious about what has to change? How many inhumane wars, oppressive taxes, poverty and crimes are we to endure before we say enough is enough? Can you name one politician or commentator who has a new path or solution who demonstrates integrity?

Remember back in grade school being told by our teachers that we should strive to be on our "best behavior" all the time. It made students feel like the kind of people they were and the kind of community they were to live in was important. Unfortunately, it was just another con-job. What I slowly came to realize, it's all part of a deliberate scam. What our teachers failed to do was define what "best behavior" means. Oh we were told to be nice, get along, don't get into fights, be honest, obey the rules, do your homework and oh-yes—shut up. Starting in the first grade, students were taught to live dependent on the government (public education) because we are presumed so flawed that we cannot trust in ourselves to be responsible for our most basic needs. In other words, whatever it is, ***it's not our fault***. There is no personal responsibility. When there's a problem it's the System that failed us. It's up to government to care for citizens. This contempt for people was and remains, deliberate, a matter of educational and cultural policy. It's how they, the emperors up on stage, keep us living as obedient doormats. It means instead of living with respect for one another we are taught to live reliant on rule makes, subservience, dependency—on the use of force if any of the nation's problems are to be solved. It is a secret plan to keep us all dependent on the powerful who insist on ruling our lives. And "best behavior" remains a vague generality. And politicians continue to promise that they are going to solve all our problems. Are we really that gullible?

We don't need to live as mindless consumers focused on making and spending money. Money and consumption are not what life should be all about. Personal character is what we should be focused upon. Having a fancy car would be far less important than caring for one's family.

Life is about more than having a wide screen television and having the latest high-tech smart phone. The good news is life sustaining values are neither complicated nor difficult to define and live by. So let's answer the question that any grade school teacher should have answered: What does "best behavior" and striving to be "the best we could be" mean and require of each of us? Or, put another way: If you want to build a better future what kind of shared expectations do we have to teach and revere? It should be clear, IF we want to restore personal liberty, we have to restore people's trust and confidence in one another and in ourselves. It is personal confidence and valid convictions on which our future must be built.

I want to welcome those who are seeking a new path, who want to address the underlying problem, to explain, validate, demonstrate and build on the ideals on which everyone's future absolutely depends. We all want to avoid and prevent disasters. You want to pursue your happiness. You want to be proud of the kind of person you are. You want to do the right thing for your loved ones. Most of us would find getting up in the morning a whole lot more motivating if we were confident that we have eliminated the possibility of civil and economic collapse.

Let's take off the blinders. Mark Twain clearly understood what we each have to recognize. Just like Socrates who recognizes the will power and potential within each of us. Here is Mark Twain recognizing the same awareness, understanding and confidence.

> Each must for himself alone decide what is right and what is wrong, and which course is patriotic and which isn't. You cannot shirk this and be a man. To decide against your convictions is to be an unqualified and inexcusable traitor, both to yourself and to your

country. If you alone of all the nation shall decide one way, and that way be the right way according to your convictions, you have done your duty by yourself and by your country--hold up your head! You have nothing to be ashamed of.
— Mark Twain, 1835-1910

We have to stop living on the backs of our children and grandchildren. Instead of relying on forced obedience we have to recognize that people and communities succeed by making healthy choices NOT by how well we obey and submit. It is within each of us to forge a new path.

I am going to define the two core values essential to solving problems instead of kicking the can down the road. Notice that none of these qualities of character rely on rules, legislation, government, or mandatory sacrifices. Here are the personal convictions necessary to hold up your head, pursue your happiness, to live as *problem solvers* instead of as *subjects* and *victims* of the insidious corruption.

First: We have to live, work and solve problems in reality. There is no make-believe world. We exist in reality and all success and problem solving means that which over time works in reality (and in harmony with nature). Our success is a result of our integrity. Our failures are the result of making excuses, trying to look good while claiming our problems and failures are someone else's fault and then believing in the nonsense that government will solve all our problems.

Honesty requires that we answer the challenge or question being addressed. It means that every argument we make must enable a solution to the problem. What does the pursuit of happiness mean: turning our backs, making excuses, sitting in front of the television, eating junk food, living on welfare and dumping our trash into the environment?

The *pursuit of happiness* and recognition of *inalienable rights* are great but: we have to live in harmony with nature, reality, our fellow humans and stop ignoring the consequences of our self-destructive habits that are making us sick, obese, pathetic—a nation of bullies and parasites.

Respect means *everyone* has the right to live without fear of being denied their natural rights and, therefore, we must not tolerate the use of force, fraud or intimidation when dealing with our fellow citizens. That respect for people to live *self-reliant* is what our founding fathers recognized. Respect defines how we want to be treated and, therefore, how we will treat others. We want to be a positive influence and contributor to our loved ones, neighbors and fellow citizens. We have to trust and respect each other by taking responsibility and standing up to the con-artists and emperors who claim they have all the solutions. Authoritarian government is manifest disrespect for citizens and their natural rights.

The virtue of *honesty*

We have all witnessed the consequences resulting from the failure to take control of one's life; *lying* to deceive someone for ill-gotten gain, or harmless fun, or on occasion to protect the innocent. But when dishonesty becomes habitual it undermines the integrity necessary to living healthy lives and live in peace with our fellow humans. Habitual dishonesty means becoming addicted to bad habits, fancy excuses and self-destructive subservience. The result, we become addicted to a culture built on promises that are propaganda, a free ride, a welfarepatricidal-subsidies-taxation system *because* we don't want to be honest.

Whether socialist or corporate-capitalist ideology, without a moral compass it means pursuing goals while refusing to acknowledge the consequences such as mindless consumption, environmental pollution, needless wars, and ignoring the collapse we are headed into. Apparently, two-hundred million citizens, or more, love such blindness because it relieves them of any personal accountability. They vote for democrats and republicans over and over. Bad habits would include texting while driving or banking policies that leads to economic collapse. Or eating a big Mac, fries and drinking a coke because we love it. Or, taking out a home mortgage without ever having to show we have any reliable income. Today we are addicted to both conservative and progressive excuses. We have become a misguided, mediocre, headed down a slippery slope nation because we have been so degenerated and abused into what may be described as living on delusional ideologies. We have been brain-washed into believing that personal convictions cannot be relied upon to solve the challenges life throws at us. We have bought into the presumption that, yes there are societal problems, poverty, inequality, terrorists but *it's not our fault*!

To illustrate the fog we now endure, you won't find personal judgment, coping with reality, or solving problems as part of the definition of honesty in any dictionary because the rule-makers DO NOT want people exercising judgment, solving problems or working in cooperation with one another. We have got to wake up: Success requires a shared *vision* on which to build a future or we are lost without knowing what to do differently. That is what *honesty* makes possible, taking control of our lives and knowing how to live as competent adults, caring for our loved ones instead of living on subsidies and putting our children deeper in debt.

Here is the current definition of honesty.

> **Honest** *1. Not lying, cheating, stealing or taking unfair advantage, honorable, truthful, trustworthy. 2.a. Not characterized by deception or fraud; genuine. b. Not calculated or constructed to defraud. 3. Equitable; fair.*
> — The American Heritage Dictionary, Published 1969-1978

What essential information is missing from this definition? How about the recognition that "honesty" has to represent and correspond to reality as accurately as possible. And surprise, we are capable of comprehending reality. Based on what I see happening we have degenerated into pragmatism, doing whatever one wants while ignoring the consequences. It should come as no surprise, because of the boredom, servitude, corruption and loss of hope the second highest cause of teenage deaths today, after auto accidents, is drug over dosing and suicide.

Look around you. We are living in a culture where lying, cheating, stealing and taking unfair advantage are common. Need I remind you we now live in a culture that has put our children trillions of dollars in debt? Such deliberate corruption, and yes it is deliberate, is an example of systematic *lying, cheating, stealing or taking unfair advantage* because such vagueness is what we have been taught to rely on. And there is no plan to reverse this descent into ever increasing national confusion. If CEOs, politicians and bankers cannot be honest with the people they serve, what kind of people are they? And what kind of people are we? If they had admitted: *we are going to put your children trillions of dollars in debt and take us into needless wars,* would we have elected them? But we did elect them and over and over. Guess what, **IT IS OUR FAULT!**

The question is how do we distinguish valid principles from fraudulent ideologies used to manipulate the listener? Is the crucial information being provided? Is the goal of the commentator to solve the problem or perpetuating the confusion to satisfy the emperors up on stage? To be honest an answer has to provide the vital information, or it's a fraud.

The current definition of honesty allows those in power to claim almost anything as true, fair, honest, compassionate, equitable, and genuine. Leaving out the crucial information is current standard operating procedure. It means compassion can mean mandated national health care and human rights can mean denying women control over their own reproductive choices. It can mean punishing whistle blowers for exposing the truth. Modern discourse represents *looking good* while taking a community into a *catastrophe*. Today we're supposed to trust and believe these leaders because they have our best interest at heart. They claim to be competent, motivated, loving, dedicated leaders promoting hope and change and we believe them. It represents spin used to deliberately conceal the Authoritarian System, mindless consumption and public policies that are inherently destructive.

We must take back control of our lives. We must stop being tolerant or involved in the on-going corruption. We must teach and practice a shared set of convictions instead of relying on bad habits, spin, and rule makers. We must build the castle on the hill on a solid moral foundation. We now live in a mental fog claiming that we are doing the right thing but never taking time to define what "right" and "wrong" means.

To give our children a moral compass that keeps them on the path to success we need to define "honesty," "integrity," "best behavior" and a "moral compass" that provides specific, real, tangible, valid, and concrete guidelines; the knowledge necessary to grow up and become the best we should be. We can restore our children's future. We can make America the most admired, trusted and loved nation on the planet.

There is no short cut, free ride, promise land, or divine rule maker. We cannot create wealth by printing money. We cannot exercise honest judgment by remaining silent or living obedient and subservient. Everything we believe and every choice we make has to be evidence of our integrity. ***The virtue of honesty is what makes us human.*** Every piece of knowledge and every argument, first and foremost, must strive to make healthy choices solving the challenge at hand.

But being honest is more than just coping with reality. People solve problems every day. People make healthy choices ninety-percent of the time. What they are not doing is defining how they judge the goals, ideals, values, promises, and the results. Driving around in cars polluting the environment means we just don't care. We are the problem because we have no commitment or values to judge our choices, solutions, means, or goals. We live and treat people like doormats because we don't want to face the truth. We live in a mental fog because we like going shopping and watching entertainment that is demeaning, filled with violence and nonsense.

Once you start to understand what honesty means you will be able to detect dishonesty in everyday life. You will learn to recognize the fraudulent in every argument and ideology you encounter. You will be able to distinguish integrity from the fraudulent in just a few sentences. It will give life a whole new meaning and confidence in each other and our selves. You will build confidence with those you work with based on everyone's commitment to solve the problems and challenges facing your family, fellow workers, and community. People will resolutely reject living helpless as slaves and peons. We will stop living dependent on government bureaucrats, welfare, needless wars, militarized police, bailouts and subsidies. We will start to demand integrity from ourselves and those around us. In a relatively short time we would be living in a whole new kind of world.

Such goals and aspirations requires that we each be prepared to talk to one another and to validate every choice we make. That is what *being human* and *best behavior* means and requires. To function as an adult we have to work together by defining shared convictions, respon-sibilities, goals, expectations and aspirations—which means *love of life* and the *pursuit of happiness*—and stop making excuses.

The virtue of *respect*

Respect for one another is the other painted line or guard rail necessary to keep us on the road to success. And just like the virtue of honesty, respect is easy to understand and apply to our everyday lives. And just like honesty the meaning of respect is largely ignored and twisted to keep us helpless and subservient. Respect answers, addresses, and makes very clear how we want to be treated and how we should treat one another. This essential virtue suffers from the same on-going mushy thinking. Here is the current definition of respect.

Respect 1. To feel or show esteem for; to honor. 2. To show consideration for; avoid violation of; treat with deference. 3. To relate or refer to.
— The American Heritage Dictionary

What vital info is missing from this definition? How about the idea, shared conviction, that we do not resort to force, fraud or intimidation to take advantage?

The opportunity of life means we want to live in a community where everyone benefits from their efforts and accomplishments without fear of being assaulted, robbed, or molested. When in a room full of people we would NOT pick the pockets of other people and they, in turn, will NOT pick your pocket. In other words, respect means we do not rob, steal and plunder, or resort to fraud, intimidation or fancy excuses to get ahead or take advantage. If someone dropped their wallet or purse we would pick it up and return it to them. We would not justify stealing claiming we are helping the less fortunate or needy. If some CEO claimed that their only responsibility was to increase share holders profits, we wouldn't do business with them. If some corporation is polluting the environment or selling fraudulent products we wouldn't buy into their scam. We would not work for or do business with a company that pays its employees slave wages. The goal and purpose of our lives and those we work and do business with is to achieve success built on respect for everyone because we want to make the world a better place. Again, that should be our shared highest ideal—making the world a better place.

What went wrong? We celebrate our commitment to personal values and then voters expect government to pick the pockets of every America—to rob, steal, plunder, and intimidate. Talk about cultural bankruptcy. We embrace taxes, welfare programs, regulations, bureaucrats, intimidation, massive prisons, bank bailouts and foreign interventions that contradict the principles we claim to revere. Today every problem is solved through the use of coercion, force and social mandates with complete disregard for the respect and solutions that we should stand for. Today the problem is: Every problem is to be solved through force and intimidation. It's not working. And increasingly people feel so left out, betrayed and so abused they are resorting to protests, violence, drugs, and suicide.

The founding fathers set forth government that was to protect people, not threaten them. In stark contrast today, we're told (promised) everything is about how government is going to solve our problems. The only responsibility we have is to pay taxes and obey the bureaucrats. The expectation of people to exercise control and responsibility does not exist in our culture any longer. The acceptance of the notion that government should provide for people's retirement, health care, education and financial aids, and be the police of the world is exactly the opposite of the kind of respect that a healthy community and world peace must be built upon. There is *no future* living as obedient sheep, doormats being walked on, and as a world empire. Respect means we live as nature intended as rational beings exercising integrity, dealing with the world around us and not as bullies and parasites.

Simply stated, we live in the one country dedicated to personal liberty and have now abandoned any commitment and regard for those ideals. Today, government is viewed not as the *protector of our rights* but as the *authority and supreme ruler* everyone must obey and rely on— institutionalized subservience, a massive prison system and regulation of virtually every aspect of people's lives and business.

Respect means we do not cooperate with those who abuse and ignore people's rights. It's pretty elementary but you will not find coherent definitions of *respect* and *honesty* in your dictionary, or taught in our schools, or practiced by our legal system. What we teach is that robbing thy neighbors to provide for everybody's needs, spreading military globalization, corporate subsidies and bailouts and being convinced that such mandatory sacrifices are all morally justified. It's a scam.

The growing national debt and oppressive taxes are evidence that we don't have any shared convictions about how to respect one another. Today taxes consume over half the average family budget. Total government spending (federal, state and local) represents 25-percent of GDP—$41,000 per household, 2011 (2016 it's around 35-40%). We will recover our hard earned money and get the thousand pound gorilla off our backs and treat people with respect only when we choose to stop living dependent on compulsory extortion, militarism, fake money, debt, subsidies and fancy excuses.

We live in a country that celebrates its love of freedom and then on a daily basis does exactly the opposite—that enslaves everyone. We are the leaders of the free world who, apparently, will not practice what we preach.

Manifest in the *Declaration of Independence* is a very simple message: *People should not and need not live as obedient subjects.* Today, if you look at what is happening, at how we conduct our public policies, the message is: *We intend to live as subjects, obedient and subservient to a welfare/warfare state.*

This is not the first time mankind has been faced with collapse.

They take our very flesh, and they hate and despise us. And who shall say we are worthy of more? When a government becomes powerful it is destructive, extravagant and violent; it is a usurer which takes bread from innocent mouths and deprives honorable men of their substance, for votes with which to perpetuate itself.
— Marcus Tullius Cicero, 106-43 B.C. Roman Statesman, Philosopher and Orator

That was 2000 years ago. We are headed for collapse for much the same reason the Roman Empire collapsed. The problem, then and now, no one wants to talk about either the real problems or the solutions. The question I am posing: *Are you prepared to have the discussion about what kind of nation and people we should be?*

When faced with criminal behaviors and crimes against humanity we must refuse to remain silent; refuse to cooperate; refuse to be complicit in the inhumanity. Living as "people" is what a free society was intended to represent. Whether it's terrorist, criminals or corruption of any kind, we have to talk about what is undermining our prospects for enduring peace and prosperity. It will require some degree of courage but we really have no other choice. We must build bridges instead of walls. People must define and revere the values, convictions and principles on which human success depends. Or the problems are only going to grow worse. If we truly want to become the most trusted, admired, loved people on earth we have to stand for our principles instead of relying on forced obedience and acting as the emperors of the world.

Young people this book is about your future. You need to understand those teachers, professors, politicians and commentators deliberately rely on spin and flawed ideologies instead of how to achieve genuine pride and confidence. They do not want you to question the meaningless debates, reporting and education that you are being subjected too. You're being lied too because it's your choices and money that they what to maintain control of. I repeat: It is your life they want to keep control of. That is why government is spying on all of us. What they secretly (or not so secretly) intend to preserve is the System that benefits the welfare-military-corporate-subsidies complex.

Your opportunity of life is what America was supposed to represent. Instead today you live in a society where you will be used, abused, enslaved, serve in the military, bearing the burdens that my generation so relentlessly imposes with no apologies. It has got to stop and only by standing up to the corruption will we turn the lights back on in America.

Two

Light at the end of the Tunnel

The mass of mankind has not been born with saddles on their backs, nor a favored few booted and spurred, ready to ride them legitimately, by the grace of God.
— Thomas Jefferson, 3rd US President

Insanity: doing the same thing over and over again and expecting different results.
— Albert Einstein

All of us should live as *people* not as *doormats* being pushed around by those with boots and spurs. Finger pointing and laying blame are not solutions. Relying on politicians promises and expecting different results is insanity. Do you know why humanity has repeatedly descended into wars, dictators, and growing poverty? Because people didn't realize what disasters they were being lead into. The same refusal to be honest is the underlying cause of the environmental crisis. But guess what—ignorance is no excuse. There is no "enemy" that can destroy America. Our freedoms and security is being lost because we refuse to demand and respect those rights and liberties set forth by our fore fathers.

> America will never be destroyed from the outside. If we falter and lose our freedoms, it will be because we destroyed ourselves.
> — Abraham Lincoln, 16th US President

We should live in a free society for one very simple reason. Human nature requires people to take responsibility for everything we say and do. We have to reject reliance on force and lies as how we deal with one another. If we want to live as responsible adults we have to learn, validate, teach and revere those personal expectations and shared principles that make human success unstoppable.

I like to think that back during the decline of the Roman Empire there were citizens who saw what was destroying their lives and desperately wanted to make the necessary changes. The problem was no one listened; or, they were brutally assaulted by government agents to keep protesters, whistle blowers, and citizens silent and obedient. For decades after the fall of the Roman Empire people longed for its return because the civilization provided something healthy, life loving people wanted and cherished. What I see today is essentially the same thing happening. There should be no doubt the same kind of blindness, lack of leadership and being assaulted by government agents IS leading to inevitable collapse.

Here is some evidence of why we are rendered so gullible. Here is an example of the mentality (flawed moral presumptions) we live with today that are the opposite of what being human requires.

> .....producers and non-producers are required to help the "Others." Government is the enabling instrument to bring out the caring tendency of people who do not know each other. To attain minimum standards of decency as a right for people rather than as a voluntary gift to them. In other words, the

government serves as a redistributive mechanism that stops the society from flying apart for economic reasons.
— Marcus G. Raskin, *The Common Good: Its Politics, Policies and Philosophy* (1986)

When reading the above quote what do you think about it? Do you agree? Do you support mandatory sharing? How do you think we should care for the "others"? What do you think the proper role of government is?

There are no emperors or bureaucratic system that relieves us of having to exercise personal judgment. What the above quote is promoting is mandated sharing *to attain minimum standards of decency*. The thousand pound gorilla we live with today is the result. The erosion of the American dream is the consequence of believing that humanity requires mandatory sharing which means— forced obedience.

The presumption, we are taught, is that people cannot manage their own lives and make healthy choices or even define a set of moral values. Thus, we must live reliant and subservient to oppressive authority—*to attain minimum standards of decency*—because we are such dolts. That is the mental cloud we now live in.

Here is a Harvard professor that has nothing but contempt for personal liberty.

I do not think that freedom of choice—even freedom of choice under fair conditions—is an adequate basis for a just society.
— *Justice: What Is the Right Thing To Do,* Michael J. Sandel (2009) professor at Harvard University. His course on "*Justice*" is one of the most popular and influential at Harvard

The real problem is not just that professors hold such contempt for human rights but that most of them do not even believe that there are definable principles that should be guiding people's lives. They actually believe that people cannot reasonably expect to solve problems. In their judgment, only benevolent government can guide and sustain civilization. It's time to face the truth; the silence, the lies, the refusal to acknowledge what benevolent government means, results in, ever growing decline in the ability, determination and right to make the most of one's life. It is everyone's pursuit of happiness that is being compromised.

According to modern philosophy the very idea that you and I are capable of defining principles, a constitution, shared values, living together with respect and compassion, does not exist in human nature.

Scientists do not disagree about the validity of specific laws that have been established, nor do mathematicians disagree about the validity of specific theorems. But there is not a single piece of philosophical knowledge, not a single philosophical proposition on which philosophers are all agreed. If progress is measured in the same way as it is in fields like medicine or physics, by increase in systematized knowledge and control, then we must acknowledge that there has been no progress. It envelopes even those who, on skeptical or meta-ethical grounds, have concluded that philosophy has nothing cognitively meaningful to say about human values.

— Sidney Hook, *Philosophy and Public Policy,* Southern Illinois University Press. Sidney Hook was an Emeritus Professor of Philosophy at New York University and Senior Research Fellow at the Hoover Institution.

You now live in a society where highly respected professors teach that:

- ☐ To achieve justice and equality we must confiscate people earning and redistribute the wealth.
- ☐ That self-realization, personal convictions and respect for people is unworkable.
- ☐ And, modern philosophy has nothing meaningful to recommend when it comes to human values.

DUH. Do you think a community can prosper without agreement on basic moral values? Isn't that what *America* was supposed to represent—a set of values? Maybe the blindness is a consequence of the choices we have made and now we have to re-examine those fallacies and ideologies? That is why I want to live in a free society where people recognize the need to talk to one another. Instead we are so demeaned, mistreated and presumed so incompetent that we must live as subjects of the anointed rulers in some kind of fantasy land. And anyone who dares to speak out against the oppression and corruption may end up imprisoned, or hiding is some foreign country to avoid U.S. prosecution. It gets worse.

> The things for which people are morally judged are determined in more ways than we first realize by what is beyond their control. And, when the seemingly natural requirement of fault or responsibility is applied in light of these facts, it leaves few pre-reflective judgments intact. Ultimately, nothing or almost nothing about what a person does seems to be under his control.

— *Moral Questions* by Thomas Nagel, professor of philosophy at New York University and author of several works in moral and political philosophy

What this professor is saying is that people (all of us) are not capable of making "moral judgments." We're supposed to believe that ***nothing*** *about what a person does seems to be under his control.* This means we are by nature helpless dolts. Modern philosophy has no vision, or principles, or values, or confidence in people. That is the underlying problem. How can we claim to be competent adults if we cannot define solutions to the growing inhumanities? Today, we are taught that we cannot be trusted, that we are not capable of exercising personal integrity because there are no qualities of character that we should revere, teach and practice in our lives. The lack of trust in ourselves means we must live winging-it or as subjects of some master authority to guide us through life because of our inherent incompetent.

What must a brain do in order to believe a certain statement is true or false? We currently have no idea. We cannot live by reason alone.
— Sam Harris, *The End of Faith: Religion, Terror, and the Future of Reason* (2004)

We do not know, nor have we ever known, whether we are right or wrong. Life's great uncertainty principle is that no one can ever be sure whether he is ultimately correct or incorrect in his views of the nature and purpose of life in the universe.
— Kalman H. Silvert, *The Reason for Democracy* (1977)

The issue that underlies our politics and our society in the 1990s is the moral, social and cultural erosion of the past quarter century in American life. It is the gradual disappearance of safe streets, stable families, secure employment, and the enduring relationships with relatives, neighbors, merchants and co-workers that make an orderly life possible. It is the unraveling of the strands of community—of what we are now calling civil society. There is no easy way to reverse it. Government cannot order moral revival. But some policies are worse than others. Entrusting our future to an uncontrolled and amoral free market may be the worst of all. Nor does it make much sense to pronounce the word "choice" over and over like a mantra. Communities aren't built on individual choice.
— Alan Ehrenhalt, *The New York Times,* Nov. 19,1995

Let's be clear, if personal liberty, or a laissez-faire economy, democracy, or a republic means living without any personal values, chaos will indeed be the result. The lesson we must learn is no amount of government or freedom or free markets *relieves us of the need for moral values*. Freedom, in fact, recognizes the need for values, principles and ideals as the foundation of our success. Freedom and the free market are NOT an escape from personal responsibility. Freedom is the recognition that ONLY by teaching basic moral principles and taking responsibility will a nation assure enduring success.

The essential threat, the true and genuine threat at the heart of all the others, is the threat to the individual. This fact often remains unseen and unremarked. We are, after all, or we once were, said to be a nation of individuals, to value individualism, to pride ourselves on our individuality, and we live, of course, in a nation whose founding was dedicated to the protection of individual freedoms. But so much of that has now been eroded, so much of it has been

Who Is Destroying Your Future?

make a sham, so much has been bent, twisted, numbed, used, channeled, undervalued, pandered to, fawned over, flattered, demeaned, made un-self-conscious, programmatically under-nourished, and again and again and again, so endlessly and unremittingly exploited as an easy means to ever baser and baser and baser ends—that the damage, if nothing else, has grown to the point of having become threatening to the nation's very life.

— Erick Larsen, *A Nation Gone Blind: America in an age of simplification and deceit,* p-127, (2006)

How does it feel to be presumed so incompetent that we must live dependent on a welfare state? How does it feel to be told the only way to provide affordable health care is if it's provided by tax-payers? How does it feel to live in a country that believes the only way to protect and preserve civilization or world peace is with a hundred military based around the globe and a thousand nuclear bombs ready to be launched? How does it feel to be living as obedient servants of the military, industrial, corporate, welfare complex? A nation that spends ten times as much on military arms than any other nation, that has the highest imprisonment of any other nation, means we are a nation in the process of cultural collapse? If we cannot or will not talk about how to assure meaningful values and long range convictions, then we are living in a moral fog.

The following quote is a columnist who describes the current inability to talk about or reach agreement on anything.

Secularists who insist that the questions of morality be answered on the basis of "reason" are merely using a different word to describe what self-consciously religious people call "the moral law" or "God's will," or something similar. And since secularists are no more able to agree upon what "reason" requires in regard to controversial moral issues than religious people are able to agree on the substance of the moral law or God's will, invoking reason when arguing about subjects such as abortion is exactly as useful as invoking the authority of sacred scripture or of the pope – which is to say, such invocations will be quite effective in convincing those who already agree with the speaker, but will otherwise fall upon deaf ears.

— Paul Campos, *Rocky Mountain News*, January 22, 2002

Paul Campos is right. What are the prospects of a community working together to solve problems if people cannot communicate or agree on anything? What kind of world will we endure if we cannot talk to one another? And by "talk" I don't mean laying blame, pointing fingers or kicking the can down the road. I mean articulating the *vision* and *principles* on which our children's future absolutely depends.

Being focused on left verses right and progressives verses conservatives is part of the problem. It doesn't matter which side wins, the problems, pollution, disparity endless wars just persist. There is no middle ground that will solve the growing inhumanities. We are standing on the decks of a sinking ship and it is my generation that has brought us to the sorry state of affairs. If the problems we now face were understood by the vast majority we would be solving the un-necessary human suffering that now confronts us. In other words, IF we practiced and agreed upon an accepted set of valid principles we would not be confronted with such doubt about our future. Human success is not found in some mythical ideology or some convoluted, slanted political agenda. Human success and personal character is just as real, definable and important as any other subject. But we don't talk about or teach an inspiring vision, or recognize the need for agreement about what matter most to achieve enduring success.

> Without a definition and identifiable grounds for morality, belief in the relativism of values and nihilism were encouraged. Morality was simply relative to each society and each person. It was either an expression of personally chosen moral beliefs or merely an unpredictable and individual expression of emotion. In either case, no basis exists for people to reach common moral understandings.
> — Norma Haan, Eliane Aerts, and Bruce A. G. Cooper, *On Moral Grounds: The Search for Practical Morality* (1985) New York University Press

That's right, today no promise or commitment exists of the need for people to reach moral convictions. But guess what. Humans are capable of living as problem solvers. I see people making intelligent choices every day, but what I came to realize, to achieve personal liberty, or to behave as problem solvers, people have to know what being good, just, fair and, most important, what human nature and living in harmony with nature means and requires. And once we learn how to live as problem solvers those emperors are going to get laughed off the stage. Top down management will be recognized for what it is—an assault on our inherent rights, on self-realization, on our confidence, potential and convictions.

As an example, what about the never ending debates on abortion? Do pregnant girls and women have the right to terminate a pregnancy? If women have a right to their life, liberty and pursuit of happiness, absolutely, they have the right to manage their own choices about giving birth. Well then, what about the unborn baby's right to life? We have a right to life. Who decides when a life begins—the pregnant woman or politicians, supreme court justices, or religious gurus? If women do NOT have that right then all of us are being treated as obedient subjects. A million people would agree that at birth *life* has begun. Before birth it is the pregnant women's right to decides if life has begun. Which kind of world—with or without basic personal respect—do you want to live in?

Where does the vision and shared convictions start? Freedom means people have the right to manage their own lives. Do they need a set of valid moral ideals to guide their choices?

Most of us want valid and inspiring education. Most of us know technology has enabled us to put a man on the moon. But what values should guide how we make choices? Do such values even exist and, if so, where do they come from?

As we enter the twenty first century there is no agreement on "right" and "wrong." We need to understand, there is no crystal ball, political system or ideology that relieve us of answering those questions. Today, there is not only no agreement, there seems to be a mindset that we cannot or **should not** teach moral values in our schools. Don't you think we should be teaching some basic ideals and vision of what America was supposed to stand for? What if the moral blindness is the yellow brick road that leads to increasing inhumanities? So let's do what healthy adults must do, lets answer the question. There are several possible answers.

Either moral values are handed down from above (over which we have no control); imposed by some master authority (over which we have little control); or they are discovered, tested, proven, articulated and validated by mankind through the reasoning process (over which we have total control). You may disagree with this analysis but you deserve to at least consider the possibility that personal convictions and self-realization are *entirely within our capability and responsibility.* And if we don't answer those questions we are admitting that, I and everyone must live as subjects of our anointed masters.

Knowledge and personal convictions are acquired through the reasoning process. We question, test, verify, and repeat the thinking process every day. For those adults who are turned off by such personal accountability the question then: Are you willing to talk about how our beliefs and values are tested and proven? Can we agree on what is means to live as problem solvers? If people are not capable of defining the principles they trust in, then how can they be held responsible or accountable? What does being "human" mean? What is the truth? How do we know? Do we really believe we *cannot* answer those kinds of questions? If we presume that our moral values are dictated to us then there is no reason to talk to one another about the most important subjects in life. If the definition of "marriage" must be dictated by religion or government then apparently we have no choice but to live as subjects. Is "life" a product of personal choices or a matter of unquestioned obedience?

Is morality something outside our own nature and judgment? If you choose to believe in living dependent, subservient and obedient that is your choice. Do you decide how you will live or do you just obey (when you feel you have too) the rules and rule makers? Is playing the system what life should be all about? The underlying question is: What does personal responsibility mean? In today's world, there is no answer or agreement to that question.

That is the underlying flaw in our country—there is NO agreement on what values would inspire and release the human potential within all of us.

We need to face the possibility that all the suffering we currently endure is a consequence of flawed moral premises and not some affliction that renders humanity doomed. My point is: *We can choose to live as competent humans.* Thus, we must define those flawed assumptions and articulate the moral values that make possible human success. We should have had this discussion a hundred years ago, but better late than never.

And here is the problem. If we don't have this discussion and define that moral compass then we are left guided by what? What if without convictions we will ultimately—fall for anything?

One view of civilization rests on a basic respect for the rights and responsibility of people to manage and provide for their needs and welfare. I call it living as "people." The other view assumes people should rely on benevolent rule makers. I call it living as "doormats." One defines the foundation of a free society; the other the justification for mandated subservience. Today, both conservative and progressive ideologies insist we live as obedient cogs in their grand plans—dependent on top-down management. America was supposed to represent the rights of each to their own life. Our intellectual leaders have compromised those ideals over the past decades so that today it is almost impossible to find a politician, author or commentator that can explain how qualities of character are THE FOUNDATION of human success.

People are capable of living moral lives and making healthy choices. Contrary to what we are taught, people are not inherently helpless, evil, or flawed, and therefore, dependent on obedience to some authority. People are capable of exercising responsibility. People don't need forgiveness or salvation, or submission to a bunch of bureaucrats. What they need, *desperately,* is *respect* for their potential and the *knowledge* on which to build self-confidence. Self-doubt is what renders people irresponsible, bored, disobedient and inclined to live as subjects with a lack of personal confidence and motivated only by taking advantage and playing the system. Guess what, personal inspiration and convictions are the guiding light of people of character. A moral compass that recognizes the human ability and potential to live as competent humans IS the prerequisite to achieving the best within each of us. To reverse the growing violence, we must build on respect for people instead of relying on force to compel submission.

> *A wise and frugal government, which shall restrain men from injuring one another, which shall leave them otherwise free to regulate their own pursuits of industry and improvement, and shall not take from the mouth of labor the bread it has earned.*
> —Thomas Jefferson, 1801

People do not develop qualities of character if they are taught to live obedient to some authority. Such obedience and dependency will only make people more obstinate, disrespectful, and potentially dangerous—a burden on society. Instead of living by personal judgment, people learn to use the laws, subsidies, handouts to their advantage, resulting in corporate corruption, black markets, a welfare state and organized crime. We live in a society of rules and rulers because the only recognized standards of behavior are a maze of meddlesome, subjective, contradictory policies and edicts. We have become a nation where the only "solution" is to rely on the legislation, edicts, mandates, fiat money and welfare benefits.

Only responsible adults can make a society work successfully.

Three:

What would
FREEDOM
look and feel like?

Did you know that our trust in government—that was supposed to provide the protection of the rule of law—now ignores the rule of law and impose prison sentences, extraordinary rendition, and massive spying on American citizens with no charges filed or appearance in court to justify the violations of citizens rights? It is evidence that we are headed into a police state—totalitarianism.

Those who deny freedom to others deserve it not for themselves.
—Abraham Lincoln, 1809-1865

Freedom means we trust and respect one another because those values are the foundation for the castle on the hill that motivates all of us. It means we build bridges instead of walls. It means we refuse to throw people into our prisons or threaten and bomb them and claim we are solving the problem. What we endure today is not a democracy, it is not a republic, it is a scam because there no agreement on what kind of governing we need. There are endless debates but it's all about more versus less government not what kind government and shared convictions we desperately need.

I watched a documentary but didn't get to watch all of it, but the message it illustrated was clear.

The program started with a group of natives meeting in their local forest discussing the trees that provided for their village, deciding which trees they would cut down and how to best sustain the forest that they relied upon. Then the documentary presented another meeting of government officials who were discussing how to allow foreign corporations to come in and extract natural resources which would pollute the forests and much of the natural habitat.

The first meeting of local natives is an example of a free society, how people can talk about preserving what is most important and vital to their long range welfare. It illustrates what may be defined as a *shared moral compass*—which means shared aspirations, values, goals and love of life to sustain everyone's pursuit of happiness, assure a better future for their children and make our goal to leave the world a better place. It's the exercise of personal responsibility.

The meeting of government officials and special interest advocates represents just the opposite. They deliberately did not what to talk to anyone who might stand in the way of their plans to make money. They illustrate what I call *pragmatism,* using reason to justify whatever they selfishly want (money and profits) while ignoring the inevitable consequences inflicted on the people or the natural environment. It illustrates the choices we make in our everyday lives and as a community. We either do the "good" and "right" thing or we don't give a hoot about the methods we embrace to serve our selfish interests. The path we take either leads to collapse that we can now see coming or a new path that will require putting everyone's well being above mindless consumption, servitude and greed.

Freedom means we take control of our lives and refuse to facilitate or cooperate with those who are pragmatist—who are leading us into collapse. More and more people are aware that something has gone very wrong. The recognition of the growing apprehension is everywhere.

Examples of the realization that something has gone very wrong would include.

- *America: What Went Wrong?* By Donald L. Barlett and James B. Steele, (1992)
- *Restoring the American Dream* by Robert J. Ringer, (1979)
- *Government Ruins Nearly Everything* by Laura Carno, (2016)
- *American Democracy In Peril* by William E. Hudson, (2004)
- *From Freedom To Slavery: The Rebirth of Tyranny in America* by Gerry Spence, (1995)

Let's start with an everyday example. Years ago Ralph Nader (1965) wrote *Unsafe At Any Speed.* This is an example of what freedom is all about. A book about how to make our lives better, safer, more assured and confident that we can all work for the best in each of us. That IS what freedom is all about but, starting back in 1935 and continuing ever since, we have chosen a very different path. Instead of paying close attention to everything that matters about people's lives, like wearing seat belts and auto designed for safety, two-hundred million America's emphatically said NO we are far too incompetent to be responsible, we want to live as subjects of massive government. So now we have volumes of laws and regulations, thousands of bureaucrats, militarized police and have ever since been descending into an authoritarian state. Instead of doing everything we can to build better, safer, more peace and prosperity, a better future for our children, we are headed for inevitable civil collapse. Years later it should come as no surprise that a driver stopped for having a broken tale light gets shot by the police officer. Once we choose and tolerate reliance on force, on government that regulates every aspect of people's lives, like a cancer grown, it only gets worse.

We are headed down a slippery slope because we will not be *honest* or talk about how *respect* for people must be part of our moral convictions. We now live in a society where the only solution to every problem is the use of force which means reliance on government. It's not working and only by taking back control of our lives will we restore the promise that America was supposed to stand proudly for. Ralph Nader was right to expose and talk about what we have to do to make our lives every more safe, responsible and successful. But he failed to recognize the inalienable rights and responsibilities of every citizen. We remain a part of the problem when we think forced obedience is going to relieve us of personal responsibility. We absolutely can live safe and productive lives but NOT if we continue to live as obedience subjects of authoritarian government. We will forge a new path when we start to revere and teach what life requires of each of us to understand and dedicate ourselves to doing what is "good" and "right".

In *Collapse: How Societies Choose to Fail or Succeed*, the author, Jared Diamond, describes how people, communities and cultures have survived and prospered for thousands of years and how some lasted only a few hundred years. He is asking his reader to make an evaluation of what is now happening to America and around the globe. His first examples are from the state of Montana over the past century which enjoyed a free market and industrial growth that has now degenerated into a welfare state and possible collapse. Today the citizens in Montana for every federal tax dollar they pay to the federal government get in return a dollar-fifty of taxpayer's money deemed necessary to save the state from environment and economic collapse. Collapse being caused by the mindless decisions made by the mining, lumber, and agriculture businesses over the past hundred years. In Montana the lumber business no longer exists, they cut down most of the forests. The mining business has caused extensive pollution of the rivers and water. And industrial agriculture has rendered thousands of acres of farm land useless caused largely by salinization. And much of the profits from the mining business went out-of-state to benefit the rich, instead of benefiting the citizens of Montana.

> Thus, seemingly pristine Montana actually suffers from serious environmental problems involving toxic wastes, forests, soils, water, climate change, biodiversity losses, and introduced pests. All of these problems translate into economic problems. They provide much of the explanation for why Montana's economy has been declining in recent decades to the point where what was formerly one of our richest states is now one of the poorest.
> — Jared Diamond, *Collapse: How Societies Choose to Fail or Succeed,* (2005)

The question is: Are we, the other forty-nine states, going down the same path? Are we headed for potential collapse caused by people and businesses that fail to examine what will be required for the long range success of their businesses and community?

What's interesting about his book is that it addresses the crisis that we are now faced with, talking about the need for values that must guide human behavior, concluding with the following: *"Two types of choices seem to me to have been crucial in tipping their outcomes towards success or failure: long-term planning, and willingness to reconsider those core values."* What is so mind-boggling (or typical) is the author never addresses or discusses those "core values." What if like those natives discussing how to maintain the forests to assure their future the citizens of Montana had talked about assuring their long range success and leaving a better state for their children? Could they have make healthy choices? Is our success or failure dependent on looking at the long range consequences of our choices and our core values? That is the question Jared Diamond is asking the reader to think about. Can we make choices that actually build a better world and pass on to our children prospects for an even better future? I think so.

Here a story to illustrate the choice, to demonstrate what happens when people refuse to be honest about the values and choices they are making and claim to stand for.

Imagine the Thanksgiving ceremonies back in 1823 that brought together some of the men who fought in the revolutionary war to win our freedoms along with some native inhabitants. They spent a day cooking, eating and talking. They were sitting around a campfire towards the end of the day. An Indian named Kesustra was joined by one of her students, an eleven year old who wanted to join in the conversation. There was a Colonel from the volunteer army who was going on about how they had finally defeated and out-smarted the English army—the strongest military forces in the world at that time. It was a great opportunity to sit down and talk with their new neighbors. An eleven year old saw his opening and asked his questions for the Colonel.

He asked: *Why is it after such a struggle to secure your rights and liberties and document the right of each to their life, liberty and pursuit of happiness do you insist on forcing natives who have lived here for thousands years off their lands and onto reservations hundreds of miles from home? Why do you import natives from Africa to live as slaves? Why do you treat some people with such contempt? Then the next day you preach your dedication to "love thy neighbor." How do you define neighbor? Am I your neighbor? This is a historic accomplishment to explicitly recognize the rights of citizens but then you deny those rights to those who should be your neighbors.*

The eleven year old never got an answer.

Then Kesustra, a village teacher, tried to restore the conversation. She looked into the eyes of the Colonel and said: *You and your neighbors and children may attend my school. We make it a priority to teach what competent behavior means and requires. We define what "neighbor" means and how it applies to everyone. We talk about those ideals that make the prospects for this new nation and promoting enduring peace and prosperity possible. What I and my students see happening does not bode well for the future.*

She got no response either. By 1837, 46,000 Natives from the southeast states had been forcibly relocated from their homelands. (For more see, *A Century of Dishonor* by Helen Jackson). The message is, we have to have a conversation to define and articulate a clear and honest definition of the meaning of freedom and personal liberty. We can do the right thing and live up to our promises to future generations. Here is an example.

These teachers, usually young women, braved nearly impossible conditions, including the hostility of Southern white society, from which they were often ostracized and sometimes threatened, and many utterly unprepared black students, handicapped both by the experience of slavery and by the general Southern culture in which education was by no means a high priority. W.E.B. Du Bois called the work of these white volunteers from the North the "finest thing in American history."

— Thomas Sowell, *Wealth, Poverty and Politics: An International Perspective,* 2015

Young people of America—you can restore the American Dream. The next time you join in a Thanksgiving celebration, take the opportunity to start the conversation about what matters most to everyone's future. If we remain silent or complacent then we are going down the same path into failure and collapse as every other empire in human history.

Years ago I was reading the history of the Lewis and Clark expedition (1804–1806). What I found amazing is that they came across an Indian tribe that even after being attack or assaulted (by others Indians or whites) would not retaliate. Revenge, assaults, and terrorists type behavior was not something they would engage in. They spend their time and energies focused on what their survival depended upon. They survived for hundreds of years as a self-sustaining, peace loving village and tribe. I look forward to the day when Christians, Muslims, atheists and Jews can act with the same kind of convictions to choose peace instead of wars, drone attacks, torture, and bombing villages, schools, hospitals, infrastructure and people.

Kesustra was right. What we see happening does not bode well for the future. Evidence of the underlying problem is that those watching this travesty unfold, apparently, have no clue as what to do differently. We the people of the free world resort to bombs, drone attacks and needless wars because we refuse to address the underlying problem or define a workable solution. Spending billions of taxpayer's dollars on wars, subsidies to foreign dictators, and rebuilding cities, hospitals, schools, neighborhoods we have destroyed means we are sacrificing innocent lives, making more enemies and going bankrupt. There is an alternative.

Here is an example of the kind of choices we could be making IF we chose to live in a culture that builds on core values, doing what is *good* and *right*—the American civil war.

Something like 620,000 or more people died as result of this conflict. **What if** instead our ancestors had chosen to live as "problem solvers" with moral convictions? **What if** when the southern state moved to withdraw from the union the northern states had reacted morally, with integrity?

The Northern States could have said to the Southern States, you joined this union voluntarily therefore you have every right to withdraw. But let's be clear: We the citizens of a "free" society will not do business with any peoples who engage in producing goods or services via slave labor. And, if slaves escape to the northern states they will be recognized as citizens like everyone else. When anyone pursuing these alleged slaves, claiming they were "property" and came into the free-states with the intention to kidnap or harmed any person, they would be arrested, charged with a crime, a violation of personal rights, and given the opportunity to defend themselves in court. If and when you want to re-engage in economic trade and business, to build a better future, we will welcome you back into the United States of America but *you have to make an absolute commitment to recognize and respect the rights and liberties of all people's.* We will with draw our military personal from your territory and look forward to the day when we again share and build on the principles and values on which humanity must be built. We believe you will one day choose a path of enduring peace and prosperity.

Humanity has been deceived over and over by emperors who claim that we must just obey and go down the authoritarian path and everything will be okay. But when asked what we must do to work together, live in peace, solving problems and achieve enduring cooperation the answer is mostly more laws and military interventions. We claim we admire and promote "democracy" or a "republic" but what are the prospects of humanity or freedom while devoted to top-down management?

The twentieth century represents unbelievable progress in technologies and knowledge about the nature of the world around us which mankind has tapped into to make life so much easier. But it has also been a century that was largely void of any quest for moral convictions on which humanity must be built.

Welcome to the future if our children are to have one. It's your future and your choice. There is no Emperor or legislation that is going to save us. We all must face this challenge working together. What matters are the choices we make both individually and collectively to build a better world. Our children and future generations will know what we did or failed to do. Genuine trust, respect and confidence in everyone is what "freedom" would look and feel like. Are we going to go on living as couch potatoes or stand up and do the right thing?

Four:

Economic Injustice

The off-shore tax havens of least 30 Americans accused of fraud, money laundering or other financial crimes have been unearthed in a groundbreaking report by The International Consortium of Investigative Journalists and a global consortium of news outlets. The first articles based on a cache of 2.5 million files were published Thursday, exposing secrets of more than 120,000 offshore entities -- including shell corporations and legal structures known as trusts -- used to hide the finances of politicians, crooks and others from more than 170 nations. These havens are harboring an enormous amount of money. One study estimated the total could be as high as $32 trillion. That's roughly the size of the U.S. and Japanese economies combined.
—Constantine von Hoffman, **CBS MoneyWatch**,2013

The growing poverty and disparity is no accident; it is a financial collapse unfolding right before our eyes. The three causes of the growing disparity, poverty and collapse:

(1) Massive oppressive taxes
(2) The rich hiding wealth in off shore accounts
(3) Devaluation of our currency which means more and more people live pay check to pay check without the

means to provide basic necessities for their families—food, health care, college education or a home.

Those in power manage the economy so that it has ups and downs—economic booms that lead to economic collapse. The most recent example would be the collapse of 2008 and now in 2016 the DOW Jones hit a record high. Since 2008, millions of working Americas have seen their savings disappear and mortgages collapsed. The economy has been in a slump since the last bubble and the politicians and economists want to restore prosperity. Restoration of the economy means restoring the confidence to borrow, spend, buy on credit, invest, and thereby to create another economic bubble. Why do they want the economy to collapse every fifteen years?

These financial investors want the economy to collapse. Then they make investments, buy stocks and property at deflated prices, watch and wait until the Federal Reserve and government stimulus spending begins to re-invigorate the economy increasing the value of their stocks and property. One way to increase the values of stocks and property is stimulus spending. The FED opens accounts with billions typed in the deposit column and then spends the "fake money" and 1-percent interest rates on federal funds that stimulate economic activity so business and consumers spend and prices go up. Their plan is when the economy has collapsed they make investments, then they see another bust coming they sell their stocks and hide their money in off-shore accounts.

Based on news reports the Federal Reserve in 2013 is pumping something like 80 billion dollars every month into the financial markets to boost the economy. I searched the internet, 2015, for *"FED stimulus spending"* and got the following—*the U.S. central bank appeared unfazed by* *concerns that its $85 billion in monthly bond purchases could disrupt financial markets or inflate asset bubbles.*

This means we are faced with another financial bubble, collapse, more inflation, disparity and poverty. These investors buy stocks, watching very carefully what the FED, the US government, other financial institutions and consumers are doing. Then when evidence of the next collapse, the next bubble is ready to burst, they sell their stocks and make millions. In the mean time, when the economy crashes those working folks suddenly find their saving gone, their life in ruins.

When government is feeding money into the economy is causes inflation. When investors remove money from the economy it diminishes the available capital for business investment. And when both happen at the same time, economists have given it a name, it's called "stagflation." These investors make millions and billion of profits by doing nothing constructive. It's called playing the System. Over the decades, the rich get rich doing nothing but sitting by their swimming pool drinking martinis while the middle class is slowing being destroyed. The cost of everything from health care to education goes up and up. That is why there is such growing disparity and distrust between working people and the elites. It's called crony capitalism because it's not based on sound financial policies but playing the System for ever more profits and consumption.

It is supposed to be the role of government to provide monetary and economic policies which would protect the currency and middle class financial stability. Protecting citizens from manipulation of the currency is what government is supposed to do. Such monetary reliability would give both investors and consumer confidence that long range financial security was something they could count on. Working people could put money in saving and be sure that twenty or thirty years later it would buy, be worth, the same or more when they withdraw the money. Because of fiat money and the resulting inflation, today most citizens have little reason to put money in saving and have little reason to hope for or can assure a better future for their children.

> From its creation in 1913, the most important Fed mandate has been to maintain the purchasing power of the dollar; however, since 1913 the dollar has lost over 95 percent of its value. Put differently, it takes twenty dollars today to buy what one dollar would buy in 1913.
> —*Currency Wars: The Making of the Next Global Crisis,* by James Rickards (2012)

Since the 1930's special interests in cahoots with the Federal Reserve has devaluated the purchasing power of our currency by well over two-thousand percent. It would now take 20 dollars to buy what one dollar would buy back in 1913. This means to have a minimum wage or pay check today with the same purchasing power as back in 1938, it would have to be over $15/hour. With continued fiat money ten years from now $20/hour would be required. Inflation makes life sustaining products and services ever more expensive. So more and more people end up living pay check to pay check if they have a job. The primary reason families cannot afford health care, college education, or food on the table is the devaluation of the currency— inflation. When I first bought a first class postage stamp it was 4 cents now it's over 45 cents, that's over a thousand percent increase. What should be clear because of massive government and deliberate devaluation of our currency the American people are being duped into living in a manipulated financial scam that is ultimately going to collapse.

Fiat money is a scam. Money doesn't grow on trees. Wealth is the product of creative, productive, responsible, honest effort. People and a nation cannot spend more than they produce. Those who promise economic security with more government regulations, spending, bail-outs and printed money are taking us down the yellow brick road. Money used in the production and exchange of goods and services *must* represent and maintain a reliable, consistent exchange rate. A sound, reliable currency is the foundation of economic security.

Over the next twenty years we must phase out all stimulus spending, welfare programs, fake money, subsidies, benefits and bailouts at tax payer's expense and debt imposed on the backs of future generations. We must care for the homeless and forgotten by giving everyone the opportunity to secure their financial future. We should set up local financial services to enable anyone to start their own business. To save us from the looming disaster, we must cut government spending at all levels by something like 70-percent. We must cut military spending to start with by 50-percent. Shut down the CIA. (See *Legacy of Ashes*, by Tim Weiner) Shut down all welfare and subsidies programs as humanely as possible. The only way to restore and maintain financial prosperity is for citizens to take control of their finances. If we persist in relying on excuses to evade personal responsibility it leads inevitable to bankruptcy. By phasing out these welfare, bailouts and subsidies we can get the tax rate on every working American down to less than 15 percent of their earnings. That would enable everyone to afford the kind of education, retirement and financial security that we should expect of ourselves. Such changes will not be easy but would assure long range economic security.

Between 1990 and 2000 the compensation awarded to the head of Citigroup rose 12,444 percent while that of the average schoolteacher in New York went up 20 percent. Meanwhile, 15 percent of the population lives below the (officially defined) poverty level, 5.5 million are in the criminal justice system, and as of 2002, more than 2 million are in prison—the highest per capita rate of incarceration in the world, 1 per 143.

—Morris Berman, **Dark Ages America: The Final Phase of Empire** (2006)

The alternative

We manage our finances with locally owned banks, employee owned companies, and reliable/stable currency. We buy products made locally. We do not buy high tech cell phones, fancy shoes, or base ball caps made in China or by any corporation using slave labor. We do not buy corporate manufactured food. We do not live on drugs. We do not drive around in gas guzzling/polluting autos. We do not do business with or shop at stores where the CEOs are making hundreds of times more than their employees. We do not put our saving and retirement accounts in the Wall Street stock market. We invest locally in business where we know how the company is being managed. We do not watch disgusting entertainment filled with violence and nonsense. We do not eat junk food confident that taxpayers will pay for our health care. We act like people instead of mindless consumers. *We take control and responsibility for our lives and finances because what is what we have to do.*

What are our children to think if we will not talk about those personal choices and public policies? Are we supposed to remain silent because these kinds of questions are not our responsibility? Apparently that is what our educators, commentators and news reporters would have us believe. Living in a world of *spin* is what we now endure. Reporters and commentators love to talk and talk while remaining silent about what has gone so wrong and how to restore confidence in ourselves.

Insanity is doing the same thing over and over and expecting different results. Enough is enough. What we must do is ask ourselves and the top 10-percent: Are we dedicated to making the world a better place; are we treating everyone with respect; are we polluting the environment; are we a nation of consumers motivated by making a profit while ignoring the inevitable conse- quences? It all comes down to a basic question: What do we, individually and collectively, stand proudly for?

Five:

Ideas Matter

OKAY: What Do We Stand For?

The reason we endure decades of drug abuse, alcohol abuse, crime, violence, health crisis and growing poverty is because we have been suckered into believing that the Emperor Johnston's War on Poverty, government run health care, more prisons, stop and frisk, three strikes and you're out and massive welfare programs would solve all of our problems. What we stand for is the idea that government is going to solve all our problems. What this should tell us is that we have to forge a new path starting with defining what we "should" stand for.

Let's start with the growing poverty. When I was growing up in the land of the free, I never saw anyone begging on the streets. For those who needed help there were charities that cared for the needy. Today, every time I venture out in pubic I see homeless people including families living on the streets. The causes of the growing inhumanities are not complicated. First, because of deliberate devaluation of our currency the cost of everything goes up and up. I estimate the cost increase due to deliberate inflation at about five percent per year. Second, the cause of growing poverty is ever increasing burdensome taxes and the costs of complying with all the bureaucratic regulations which means the cost of everything is going up and up. I estimate this burden imposed by taxes and bureaucracy is increasing at about three percent per year. The *War On Poverty* is just one example of how ignoring the source of the problem only perpetuates the problem. We could return to economic security for virtually everyone with a stable currency and minimal government that serves its constitutional functions. We could make the return to such core values in a few years, but time is running out. If we don't make these changes we are going to descend into financial and civil chaos. Again it is the total absence of competent leadership and the refusal to define and adhere to those core values on which civilization must be built. DUH, it not complicated. When we finally see growing confidence and determination to do what is right, we will know we have forged a new path built on valid values.

The debates over the illegal immigrants would be another example. Back in 2012 president Obama visited South and Central America where he was asked to address the drug wars killing hundreds in Mexico, Central and South America people. Our neighbors know who buys the drugs and who sells the guns to the drug smugglers and wanted to talk about the problem. The response from our president to the concerned leaders of Central and South America was—silence.

To "solve" the immigration problem we are told will require forty seven billion dollars for militarization of the Mexican border. I look forward to the day when someone stands next to the border fence and says, like President Reagan did about the Berlin Wall, "Take down this fence." When anyone builds walls and fences instead of solving the problem, its evidence that the only "solution" they know of is more threats, intimidation and military spending.

Instead we would end the war on drugs, stop supporting dictators around the globe, stop selling military arms around the globe, and start to offer education on the core values on which civilization must be built. That of course means we first have to define those core values here in our own schools and communities. In short we would start to talk to people instead of promoting violence and terrorism with our military interventions that only make matters worse. People would then start to move back to Mexico and Central American countries where their communities provided the peace and security that core values make possible. To build peace, security and trust we need to talk to one another whether our neighbor or foreigners. We must end the "axis of evil" mentality and more forward to a shared respect for everyone.

The reason so many people resort to self-destructive life styles is because they have no expectations of making something of their lives. The opportunity of life that America was supposed to represent, for its citizens, does not exist any longer which is why we have growing numbers who feel betrayed. In order to restore people's confidence we would have to restore both the opportunity of life and the knowledge and convictions on which personal ambition and confidence must be built. We would have to start to treat people as *people* instead of as subjects, doormats, and slaves.

Relying on flawed ideologies we have become used to never knowing for sure what the truth is. The result, we cannot work together to solve problems. We cannot talk to one another because each lives in his or her own liberal, conservative, progressive, oppressed, elite, six-pack guzzling, make-believe world—self-induced fog. It isn't so much that people view the world from their own perspective, but that their world is not understood or shared by anyone of different background or beliefs. People have rarely experienced the understanding and confidence made possible through honest communication.

This means America's schools do not teach the principles on which a free society rests because government run schools cannot teach that legislated obedience represents a violation of our values and principles. Rather than be honest our educational professionals remain silent. Or, they feed the indoctrination machine by teaching the need for mandatory obedience to promote the common good. Public discourse becomes a process of twisting the truth to defend the System that we should have recognized as fundamentally flawed.

A country that ignores or remains silent about the principles on which it was founded cannot teach those principles. A country that practices contradictions cannot teach the virtues of honesty, integrity, and personal convictions. A country that enslaves its citizens cannot teach respect for individual rights or demonstrate how such principles would solve the disparity that now confronts us. A country that does not revere its founding principles will grow to feel it is going down a path it never should have taken.

Six:

Legalized Theft

Thus, the State is a coercive criminal organization that subsists by a regularized large-scale system of taxation-theft, and which gets away with it by engineering the support of the majority... through securing an alliance with a group of opinion-molding intellectuals whom it rewards with a share in its power and pelf.
— *The Ethics of Liberty* by Murray N. Rothbard

However accurate or inaccurate the agency's numbers may be, tax law explicitly presumes that the IRS is always right -- and implicitly presumes that the taxpayer is always wrong -- in any dispute with the government. In many cases, the IRS introduces no evidence whatsoever of its charges; it merely asserts that a taxpayer had a certain amount of unreported income and therefore owes a proportionate amount in taxes, plus interest and penalties.
-- James Bovard (1956-) American author, lecturer. Source: *The IRS vs. You, American Spectator*, 1995

I have no problem with government providing public services but it has to be done honestly with respect for everyone. Taxes may NOT be used to finance an authoritarian state, for example, to confiscate and redistribute citizen's money. When we pay gasoline taxes used exclusively for building and maintain the roads those fees are a legitimate payment for services rendered. When government takes out loans to build roads and bridges that means they expect our children and grandchildren to pay for our highways, which is a form of extortion. Why should future generations pay for our roads? Future generations are going to have costs and expenses to maintain the roads when they grow up. We should be setting aside assets to pay for the maintenance of our roads and infrastructure. Having our children pay for our highways is typical of a generation that will take whatever it can get away with.

Democracy must not be misconstrued to mean anything voters or corporations can get away with, a free ride, bailing out business and banks, running up massive debt. Being honest people create wealth through hard work and creative inventions.

Who is responsible for the growing numbers of homeless families; businesses that aim to make a profit honestly, providing needed goods and services, OR government that confiscates half of people's earnings? Do we think we can provide for our children's future by stealing their money? Do we have the right to send the police into our neighbors' homes if we don't approve of how they are managing their lives?

In her book, ***Godless: The Church of Liberalism***, Ann Coulter asks: *But if we cannot legislate what goes on in the bedroom, why can't I hide money from the IRS under my mattress?* Guess what: As long as government is stealing people's hard earned money you should be hiding money from the IRS. Isn't that what the rich do, routinely, with crafty loopholes, corporate subsidies, and deposits in foreign banks? If the rich can hide wealth in off-shore banks why can't working Americans hide their money under their mattress?

We know why; the rule of law is slanted to protect the rich and to pick the pockets of working Americans. We are not paying for services rendered. We're playing a game rigged by politicians who serve special interests and corporate lobbyist. The reason people feel so threatened by their government is because government now represents a form of organized crime. Why are billions of our tax dollars going to fund corrupt governments and needless wars around the world to protect and subsidize corporations?

The rule of law means a legal system limited to protecting citizens from force, fraud and negligence, and not a set of laws used to rob, steal and plunder. Have you ever heard the Courts or commentators address questions like the constitutionality of a tax code that is deliberately vague; whether there is a law that requires working Americans to pay or file federal income taxes; whether the government has the right to legislate massive, socialist programs; whether the federal government has the authority to manage education clear down to the grade school level? The reason the Courts, politicians and commentators will not address such questions is because they are afraid of upsetting the groupthink mentality. Lawyers really don't know what principles to uphold or what the *rule of law* really means. Here are a few examples regarding current tax laws.

No one may be required at peril of life, liberty or property to speculate as to the meaning of penal statutes. All are entitled to be informed as to what the State commands or forbids..... That the terms of the penal statute creating a new offense must be sufficiently explicit to inform those who are subject to it what conduct on their part will render them liable to its penalties, is a well-recognized requirement, consonant alike with ordinary notions of fair play and the settled rules of law. And a statute which either forbids or requires the doing of an act in terms so vague that

men of common intelligence must necessarily guess at its meaning and differ as to its application, violates the first essential of due process of law.
— Justice Butler, *Lanzetta v. New Jersey* (1939)

The last time the Supreme Court heard an appeal for an illegal failure to file conviction (failure to file tax forms), ruled that 5th amendments rights were violated by filling federal tax forms.
— *United States vs. Sullivan*, 274 U.S. 259, (1928).

In other words:

a) The income tax is unlawful because it is vague, arbitrary, and incomprehensible and can be used by politicians to fund whatever they wish; and

b) The income tax laws violate the 5th amendment that protects people from having to provide information that may be used against them in a court of law. And our legal professionals don't give a hoot. To bypass these violations of citizen's rights, the IRS does not prosecute tax violators. Instead it confiscates people's hard earned money and property without every filing charges, taking them before a jury, or giving them an opportunity to defend themselves in a court of law. The IRS is nothing less than a form of organized crime.

Considering that senior officials at the Internal Revenue Service are fully aware of the fact that there is no law currently in existence making a U.S. citizen liable for or required to pay either the income tax or the social security employment tax, only a truly generous citizen would, upon discovering this, continue to voluntarily donate these taxes to the government by allowing them to be withheld from his paycheck on a 100% voluntary W-4 withholding agreement. But, then again, the IRS would be dead in the water without

the "voluntary (and docile) compliance" of employers and employees and has said so all along.
— William Cash, IRS Senior Manager, *Liberty-Tree.ca (2015)*

In America any taxes for purpose of *redistribute of the wealth* are illegal, especially when it steals from the poor and rewards the rich. This raises the question: Well what about progressive taxes that are lower for the poor and higher for the rich?

There is nothing immoral about a progressive tax system because the wealthy who own and manage businesses add all taxes necessary to operate their business to the cost of those products and services. Thus the citizens (consumers) who spend their earning on those goods and services are paying the taxes businesses have included in the cost of doing business. Thus, a fair income tax might be 15-precent of all earning but only for earning over $30,000 per year. Any earning under $30,00/year would go untaxed. This would motivate everyone to be productive, responsible and work to earn a living.

We can live in a society that encourages people to make the most of their opportunity of life OR one that relies on legalized coercion, servitude, massive prison system and militarized police. Put differently, do we believe we can solve problems relying or force, or do we understand that solving problems is an individual aspiration expected of everyone? Can you imagine living in a community where you never feel the need to lock your home or car? That is the kind of America I grew up in.

The following are two very different views of the Rule of Law.

Our legislators are not sufficiently appraised of the rightful limits of their power; that their true office is to declare and enforce our natural rights and duties, and to take none of them from us. No man has a natural right to commit aggression on the equal rights of another; and this is all from which the laws ought to restrain him; every man is under the natural duty of contributing to the necessities of the society; and this is all the laws should enforce on him; and, no man having the right to be the judge between himself and another, it is his natural duty to submit to the umpirage of an impartial third party. When the laws have declared and enforced all this, they have fulfilled their functions; and the idea is quite unfounded, that on entering into society we give up any natural right.
— Thomas Jefferson

A Constitution is not intended to embody a particular economic theory, whether of paternalism and the organic relation of the citizen to the state or of laissez fair. It is made for people of fundamentally differing views, and of accident of our finding certain opinions natural and familiar, or novel, and even shocking, ought not to conclude our judgment upon the question whether statutes embodying them conflict with the Constitution of the United States.
— Justice Oliver Wendell Holmes, Jr.

Thomas Jefferson is recognizing the principle that *the law* serves to protect the rights of citizens and little more. Justice Oliver Wendell Holmes, in contrast, is promoting the idea that that there are NO principles and NO limits the laws of the land should be built upon. Some ten-year-old should have informed the Justice about the closely guarded secret not talked about in the halls of government—that America stands for the rights of everyone to live free of servitude. Under Justice Holmes interpretation government thus becomes whatever people want to escape personal responsibility and rig the system we all live in. Thus congress and the Supreme Court will likely promote any interpretation of the law they choose.

If you are ever sitting on a jury, regardless of what instructions are handed down by the judge, we citizens have the right and responsibility to refuse to convict anyone for violations of laws that are unconstitutional. It's called jury nullification.

Breaking the law means any use of force, intimidation, deliberate deceptions or behavior which clearly threatens innocent people; such as driving around drunk. For example why punish someone who refused to pay income taxes, use of marijuana, providing cosmetic services without a state license, or revealing secrets of corrupt government (whistle blowers) who have the right of free speech. For example, to be legal and constitutional those income taxes must fund legitimate government. If they are funding fraudulent government then refusal to pay does not represent the use of force, intimidation, deliberate deceptions or behavior which clearly threatens innocent people. In fact, it's the government that represents the use of force, intimidation, deliberate deceptions or behavior which clearly threatens innocent people. The use of marijuana does not represent the use of force, intimidation, deliberate deceptions or behavior which clearly threatens innocent people. Government licensing of business does not serve to protect citizens, its regulation of citizens for no legitimate purpose. In a free society professions and business would form clubs or private agencies that monitored the validity and integrity of those businesses to assure their competency and reliability. Those who have not, and do not, represent the use of force, intimidation, deliberate deceptions or behavior which clearly threatens innocent people are guilty of no crime.

> Indeed, the United States now has the exact opposite of a single set of laws before which everyone is equal. It has an entrenched two-tiered system of justice: the country's most powerful political and financial elites are virtually immunized from the rule of law, empowered to commit felonies with full-scale impunity and to act without any constraints, while the politically powerless are imprisoned with greater ease and in far greater numbers than any country on the planet.
> — *With Liberty and Justice for Some*, Glenn Greenwald (2011)

> **United States v. O'Brien, 1968**
> Sustained the conviction of a young man who violated a federal law by burning his draft card, explaining that he did so in order to influence others to adopt his antiwar beliefs. The Court said that and incidental limitation on first amendment freedom is justified if (a) it is within the constitutional power of the government; (b) it furthers an important substantial government interest; (c) the government interest is unrelated to the suppression of free expression; and (d) the incidental restriction on alleged First Amendment freedoms is no greater than is essential to the furtherance of that interest.
> — Edward Conrad Smith, *The Constitution of the United States with Case Summaries*

The principles set forth in *United States v. O'Brien* suggests that if some of our young people protested the welfare state with the intent of influencing others to adopt their anti-socialist beliefs and burned their Social Security cards, they would be arrested, convicted, and thrown in jail. Expressing their right to freedom of speech and standing up for their rights means they would be prosecuted under our current corrupt legal system.

What does it means when the restriction of our liberties are acceptable when government's interest is unrelated to the suppression as claimed in *United States v. O'Brien*? Is there such a thing as First Amendment freedoms according to this ruling or are such "rights" just allegations by uninformed protestors? This ruling means being opposed to corrupt government and protesting such policies, could get you arrested and thrown in jail. Does that sound like a free society? Clearly the government that was set forth to protect us is now the institution of insidious harassment and enslavement.

Federal mandated healthcare legislation is another example. Here is a quotation from a news report about the Supreme Court's ruling (2012) on the constitutionality of national federal health care legislation. I copied this from an on-line news report. U.S. Supreme Court Chief Justice John Roberts states:

> *We do not consider whether the act embodied sound policies. That judgment is entrusted to the Nation's elected leaders. We ask only whether Congress has the power under the Constitution to enact the challenged provisions.*
> — Chief Justice John Roberts

What the Supreme Court Chief Justice is saying apparently—*there are NO principles or restraints on government that the Congress or the Courts must abide by or respect. Government and politicians may do whatever they feel is necessary or justified including government managed national healthcare; and the courts have no responsibility to hold government accountable to abide by the U.S Constitution.* That describes the insidious corruption, the moral fog we now live in.

If the country descends into a police state, our elected politicians, the members of the Supreme Court and the legal profession will declare it's not their fault; but it *will* be their fault. When the government passes laws that serve to dictate people's lives and the Courts declares them constitutional, the Court is providing the invisible thread used to make the web we are all trapped in. The rule of law has become the rule of the lawless. The only way we will restore our children's future is to restore the principles that respects and protects people's right to live as competent adults with respect for the rights of every citizen. The best kept secret in America—personal liberty and shared convictions that motivate, inspire and provide the opportunity of life that humanity depends upon are no longer recognized. The increasing numbers of protests are indicators of what is coming.

Seven:

Becoming a New Person

Your future and confidence is in your hands.

Imagine schools where the teacher keeps secret that he or she admires government welfare spending, government run education, massive military spending, drives a gas guzzling SUV, shops at a grocery to buy food laced with chemicals with little nutritional value, live at home where there is no vegetable garden, a big box energy-inefficient home, watches entertainment that is degrading and thinks government regulation of businesses and private choices are a good thing. How would such a teacher stand for or teach moral convictions or be a role model?

We can take this example one step further. When America actually starts to provide moral instruction, the students are going to want to know everything about their teachers, their convictions and values, and teachers are going to want to know everything about his or her students. Everything—what they like best about life, what values they revere, and what are their cherished goals and aspirations in life.

Why, because knowing and caring about our neighbors and fellow citizens IS the foundation of a civil society. Civil society means knowing what ideas and values people revere that holds the community together. The source of humanity is the basic respect and appreciation for our fellow citizens and the shared expectations to build better lives for everyone. How we treat one another, communicate and solve problems defines who we are. That is why ethics is vital to our success and happiness. Morality is about what kind of people and community we strive passionately for.

Throughout the course of every day we spend a fair amount of time in buildings. Man-made structures that provide a place to work together, live and study with others. Notice, while in one of those structures we all have a substantial degree of confidence that the floor under our feet and the roof over our heads is not going to collapse. We feel safe in those buildings because the people who designed and built them did so with knowledge, integrity and personal expectations. We feel safe because of the learning, skills, knowledge and dedication to a *job well done* and *best behavior*—moral values.

Quality education would build enduring confidence and trust in ourselves and one another. Character development would start at home, in community organizations where neighbors share and talk about the challenges we all face. Students would spend time addressing every question about human choices and the vision on which their communities must be built to thrive, discuss and evaluate how they would respond to challenges they were going to be faced with when out in the real world. The purpose of such discussion is to identity, test, validate, examine in every detail how to distinguish between contrived excuses versus building enduring success and self-confidence. Students would be encouraged to bring up any question or concern that they wanted addressed. At the end students would be able to identify the dishonest and fraudulent within a minute or less. They would know who was deceiving them and who they would want to work with and trust in. Most of all they would know what kind of *person* they should strive for in their lives. They would know that building a better world would be their passion. Teachers would be role models instead of disciplinarians. The result, in fairly short time the community would build trust and confidence in everyone, our leaders, and our nation that would inspire instead of demean everyone. Personal expectations would replace the boredom and lack of hope and confidence. We could be confident that every product and service brought to the market was based on personal integrity.

Here is evidence of what we endure today.

Many philosophers would say that they cannot establish correct theories about how one ought to live, because no one can do so. There is, they would say, no such thing as a "correct" view about how one ought to live, since beliefs about such matters cannot properly be said to be either true or false. Rather, they should be understood as expressions of feelings or attitudes, choices or commitments, and if people differ from one another in their basic attitudes about what is good or right, there is in principle no way of resolving the disagreement, no "correct" answer to be arrived at.

— Richard Norman, **The Moral Philosophers: An Introduction to Ethics** (1983)

Without a definition and identifiable grounds for morality, belief in the relativism of values and nihilism were encouraged. Morality was simply relative to each society and each person. It was either an expression of personal chosen moral beliefs or merely an unpredictable and individual expression of emotions. In either case, no basis exists for people to reach common moral understanding.

— Norma Haan, Eliane Aerts, and Bruce A. G. Cooper, *On Moral Grounds: The Search for Practical Morality,* New York University Press (1985)

Want to know what why we are headed down the path to collapse? Because currently: *No basis exists for people to reach common moral understanding.* And: *There is in principle no way of resolving the disagreement, no 'correct' answer to be arrived at.* This brings us back to where we started. The problem is our intellectual leaders have no respect for or confidence in the essential role that personal character provides in people's lives. If there is a problem we just legislate more rules, regulations and spend more of tax payer's money. The Emperor's Mission accomplished.

Nothing is going to change until we start to teach a set of values and ideals on which civilization must be built. Teachers and parents should express, examine, and build on those essential qualities of character. Once they do we will soon be living in whole new world.

Young people, instead of accepting defeat, regimentation, hatred and abuse talk about the problems and solutions. Teenagers should refuse to register for a Social Security number. Refuse to sit in a class room where the teacher refused to articulate or build on valid principles. What can you do to be part of the solution because the current authoritarian system is going bankrupt. This time America needs to understand what personal liberty really means instead of more talk with no substance.

To give you an example of how young people can change the world. Nine months before Rosa Parks refused to give up her seat on a bus in the segregated South and set off the civil rights movement, a fifteen year old girl did the very same thing—refused to give up her seat on a segregated bus in the racially bias South and was arrested and hauled off by the police. Mission accomplished.

Get this book in the hands of your friends. Start to talk about what has gone wrong and what we must do to save America. In a very short time, people will go back to work and bureaucrats will be out of a job. People will talk to one another instead of laying blame, pointing fingers, making excuses, kicking the can down the road and putting our children ever deeper in debt.

On September 11, 2001, the bombing of the World Trade Center, America made a huge mistake. We had the attention of the world. We had the sympathy of the world. We had the opportunity to lead the world to address the growing hatred and violence around the world. And we did exactly the wrong thing. Instead of joining in a mission to build a better world working with everyone, we proclaimed a War on Terror. We went down the reliance on force, torture, secret prisons, insidious destruction, more wars and surveillance of everyone. We again proved we don't trust anyone. We don't revere any values that we should live by or that we would recommend to anyone. We have caused the growing terrorism around the world. We have abandoned the conviction to do what must be done and instead have made more enemies.

> The ISIS propaganda strategy compels people to action: ISIS has persuaded an estimated 30,000 people from over 85 countries to travel to hostile war zones in Iraq and Syria while inspiring other supporters to commit acts of violence on ISIS's behalf in their home countries. And ISIS propaganda does not only focus on its military activity: ISIS also tries to portray itself as an effective government, but that effort rarely gets the level of attention in mainstream U.S. press that its military activity does.
> — On-line news report, August, 2016

Instead of relying on force, intimidation, bombs, drone attacks and military interventions we need to stand for something that works. Instead of sending armies to invade and over throw tyrannical governments, support and funding dictators, we need to restrain our military obsessions and send out peace advocates. These peace advocates would carry no guns, visit foreign countries, shake hands with citizens, learn about their culture and ask a very simple question: *How can we help?* And military interventions would only be allowed when done in accordance with the U.S. Constitution where only Congress can authorize any use of our military. Some peoples around the globe would welcome us as "advocates of peace and humanity." Others, authoritarian dictators, would not allow or welcome us to teach and work with them on rebuilding civilizations. But people around the globe want to build and restore their lives and communities. And, there is something very different today as we enter the twenty-first century. We could be using the internet, just as terrorists do, to share our values, convictions and respect for life around the globe. We don't have to send peace advocates. We have a means to reach people around the globe. It's called modern technology, the internet and cell phones that allow anyone to communicate with almost any one. The rulers no longer have absolute control, they have to listen to the people or *the people* will no longer tolerate or cooperate with their insidious corruption. We will restore humanity around the globe when we take back control of our lives, stand up to the corruption and share the values on which human progress must be built. We have seen the protests against oppressive, dictatorial, violent governments. The peace advocates are going to be everywhere. They are going to restore civilization by teaching the need for personal opportunity (freedom) and personal responsibility—moral convictions.

If America is going to provide leadership, promoting freedom, justice and the rule of law that respects protects citizen's rights, the first step and test is—*are we building on those ideals here in America?* If we are going to make America the most respected, trusted and admired nation on earth we have to start right here at home and build on those ideals. We have to take seriously the inherent rights for all people or the violence, poverty, wars and terrorism will continue.

We should dismantle our weapons of mass destruction; there is no foreign enemy that can subdue, defeat, or enslave America. The real threat is the enemy within—within each of us by failing to stand up and do the right thing. The problem is millions of Americans (most of who claim to love America) support, work with and live on the corruption that government now represents.

Education that defines the opportunity, expectations, convictions and principles to make the most of everyone's opportunity of life is essential. Web sites should be made available for anyone to post educational materials including character education, reading, writing, arithmetic and science classes on which human competency must flourish. Education would be available for almost everyone at very little cost. Talking about how to be the best we could be is what civilization must be all about. Education would be provided because it is the essential source of enduring human peace and prosperity. Here is a revolutionary idea—instead of being the tool for brainwashing—television programming would illustrate, teach, demonstrate, inspire and motivate the dedication and convictions on which our future must be built. We would watch programs that would illustrate how we can solve the problems we now face.

We can build a New World where our technological competence would be matched by our moral values. We can build a nation where people face reality with honesty and confidence; a world where people would act with integrity, purpose, and respect for those around them. People would not live in fear of crime, violence, and corruption. When they find something afflicting their lives or those they care about, responsible adults would find ways to address the problem rather than electing politicians who make hollow promises. Problems like cultural inequities, population growth, health care, deficit spending, corporate corruption, abortion, discrimination, drug abuse, and pollution would be addressed by each citizen as a personal responsibility. The nightly news would report on our successes instead of endless debates with no substance. The future would be in people's hands and they would respond knowing that nothing is more important than what they achieve in their lives laying the foundation for a better future for everyone.

I know this is not going to be easy; but over the next five years we have to do the right thing. If we fail then five years from now the thousand pound gorilla on our backs will be a three-thousand pound gorilla. We have to stop accepting handouts, bailouts, subsidies and welfare benefits. We must stop making excuses and refuse to live as obedient subjects on the backs of our neighbors and children.

We have to address and solve the healthcare crisis by living healthy life styles. We have to address and solve the growing disparity by managing our finances, employment and consumption (a green revolution) that builds a better world for everyone.

When parents, teachers, intellectuals and high school students can define the qualities of character required to achieve all that we want in life, the new world will be achieved. The biggest hurdle will be recognizing that it does not require more government, but requires each of us to discover and nurture the moral courage within ourselves.

Young people of America, you must correct my generation's mistakes. You have cell phones and computers but you have not been taught the virtues and values that would build a thriving middle class.

Young people you can lead the way in assuring a better future for your children. You can rise above the lies, evasions, and distortions being taught and practiced. You can break the silence and wipe out the pessimism and cynicism that hangs over America. You can lead the way out of the polluted warehouse into the light. You can become the leaders of a new world. The dawn of a new kind of civilization, with moral ideals, genuine equality and justice for all awaits your leadership. The choice is hope and success or inescapable boredom.

> Boredom is the first taste of nothingness. For boredom leads instantly to "killing time." For the bored, no action is more attractive than any other. The self cannot be drawn into action; it lives by and for distraction; it waits. The world acts; the self is acted on. Besides boredom, there is the collapse of a strongly inculcated set of values. I have heard students say with bitterness that high school is "enough betrayal for a lifetime." But after that, what? Social scientists leap in to tell the adolescent that everything is relative, that everything is determined, and to suggest that the social system is the source of his inner emptiness. It is not only the large, impersonal bureaucracy that engenders feelings of helplessness. It is also the recognition that those who wield power are also empty.
> — Michael Novak, *The Experience of Nothingness*

A country that ignores or remains silent about the principles on which it was founded cannot teach those principles. A country that practices contradictions cannot teach the virtues of honesty, integrity and respect. A country that enslaves its citizens cannot teach personal character and respect for individual rights or understand how such principles would solve the problems that now plague us. A country that does not revere its founding principles will grow to feel it is going down a path it never should have taken. A country that ignores the vital need for personal values is a society abandoning its moral foundation. That is what makes a free society so inspiring; citizens are dedicated and motivated for the good of everyone and future generations to **DO THE RIGHT THING**.

We are faced with a growing health crisis. Why? Because the health care industry, the pharmaceutical industry, the chemical producers, auto industry, petroleum industry, industrial food producers, junk food restaurants, the massive consumption businesses do not what to recognize or talk about how they benefit and thrive on what is the cause of the health crisis. We are making ourselves and everyone sick and refuse to take responsibility or look at ourselves in the mirror. Just like the looming financial crisis we live on a bunch of fancy excuses. Does anyone believe that government health care programs are going to solve the problem? Government funded healthcare is like putting a post-a-note on everyone's refrigerator—*Eat all the junk food you want, your neighbor's children are going to pay for your health care.* There are solutions that we have to implement if we are going to restore our health and save the planet. For example read, ***The Soil Will Save Us*** by Krislin Ohlson.

Thousands of years of poor farming and ranching practices—and, especially, modern industrial agriculture—have led to the loss of up to 80 percent of carbon from the world's soils. That carbon is now floating in the atmosphere and even if we stopped using fossil fuels today it would continue warming the planet. But by restoring healthy, organic farming practices around the globe we could put the carbon back into the earth where it came from, make the foods we eat healthy again by not using poisonous chemicals, and restore the water retention in our soils so that plants would have the water when they need it instead of water run-off causing floods and rising oceans.

Civilizations are NOT built on mandatory (forced) obedience of any kind. We must reject the argument that people are flawed and must live dependent on divine intervention, collective regimentation, a welfare state, or sacrificing their lives to serve the emperors up on stage. Civilization is built on the understanding that people, each of us, can be competent, proud, trust worthy problem solvers and a positive contributor to humanity.

People are capable of living moral lives and making healthy choices, living in harmony with one another and with nature. Contrary to what we are taught, people are not inherently helpless, evil, or flawed, and therefore, dependent on obedience to some authority. People are capable of exercising responsibility. People don't need forgiveness or salvation, or submission to a bunch of bureaucrats. What they need, *desperately,* is *respect* for their potential and the *knowledge* on which to build self-confidence. Hopelessness, self-doubt and boredom are what renders people irresponsible and inclined to engage in self destructive behaviors.

It is a simple but profound concept—responsible adults work together to solve problems. A free society does not coerce, compel, or intimidate; it does not provide, plan, or think for people; it protects people's right to take responsibility for their own lives, needs, welfare, and happiness. It remains a revolutionary ideal that has been the guiding light that has made America so successful.

History records everything we do as a nation. Look at every totalitarian dictatorship in history, including apartheid, racist, fascist, dictators, communist and the needless wars. They are plagues that people were led into that were entirely avoidable and preventable *had people known better*. But these plagues occurred because they were never taught what values sustain human progress. They never comprehended the personal convictions that release the human potential. Instead they believed and trusted in their rulers who turned out to be con-artists.

When public discourse looks more like a family feud instead of a process of honest communication, when we cannot solve basic problems, it is time to ask ourselves why. Why is communication a process of spin, bias arguments, subjective definitions, and proselytizing? When human discourse resembles "advertising" more than "education," how are people to develop self-confidence? Advertising aims to persuade by narrowing and distorting the subject, focusing on sound bites, to seduce people into mindless consumers. Education, in contrast, is supposed to explain, clarify and develop human abilities. Education is supposed to mean learning how to distinguish truth from propaganda, self-worth from self-abdication. Advertising is the art of misleading people with creative schemes to get everyone to buy into whatever is being sold. In contrast, a coherent argument identifies the concepts crucial to problem solving, to understanding the potential benefits of a recommended course of action. Instead, we are taught there is no such thing as personal responsibility or shared ideals we can all agree upon.

Instead of living in the gray area, remaining silent, or descending into a yelling match, start the discussion that could change everyone's lives. For parents and adults, who are still reading, you will learn things about your children you never imagined. You may discover how aware they are of the problems facing America's youth, and what kind of pain, loneliness, anger, and emptiness they are enduring. You will discover how important and essential getting in touch with personal convictions and expectations are to developing lasting personal relationships.

Friends and loved ones are far more important than money, but they do require a commitment to share the values on which relationships are built.

Families and communities require the establishment of trust and confidence that has been proven over time, based on shared values that become again and again more important than money. What is vitally important is the mutual respect and willingness to be there for someone under any circumstance. Being there for someone or for your community when they need help is a vital part of being human. Being there for people in need and exercising personal judgment built on *honesty* and *respect* are the convictions humanity requires.

Young people, if you cannot get honest answers from available adults, start your own discussion group. What is at stake is nothing less than your future. Listen to what adults, teachers, and politicians are saying. Words have meaning and convey ideas. Ideas are the building blocks to human success.

We all want to avoid and prevent disasters. You want to pursue your happiness. You want to be proud of the kind of person you are. You want to do the right thing for your loved ones. Most of us would find getting up in the morning a whole lot more motivating if we were confident that we have eliminated the possibility of civil and economic collapse. There is hope, courage and tremendous potential with-in each of us. Are you ready to forge a new path?

> If something is wrong for you or me, it is also wrong for the cop, the soldier, the mayor, the governor, the general, the Fed chairman, the president. Theft does not become acceptable when they call it taxation, counterfeiting when they call it monetary policy, kidnapping when they call it the draft, mass murder when they call it foreign policy. We understand that it is never acceptable to wield violence nor the threat of violence against the innocent, whether by the mugger or the politician.
> — Llewellyn H. Rockwell, Jr. (1944-) Chairman of the Ludwig von Mises Institute

> The capacity to exercise moral autonomy, the capacity to refuse to cooperate, offers the only route left to personal freedom and a life with meaning.
> — Chris Hedges, *The World As It Is: Dispatches on the myth of human progress* (p-85)

Our future is in our hands and always has been. We have to restore freedom in America meaning an absolute commitment to personal integrity. Integrity means human kind as the one life form on the planet which has the ability to reason, that is with every choice we make it is our moral responsibility to do what is life sustaining—what is "good" and "right". Otherwise we, and especially our children, are going to witness and endure the descent into another in a long history of collapses. Each of us are *human* and must be ***part of the solution*** based our commitment to exercise moral integrity as the guiding light in our lives.

Welcome to the future.

www.ingramcontent.com/pod-product-compliance
Lightning Source LLC
Chambersburg PA
CBHW070215290526
45789CB00002B/992